Freight Broker Business

How to Start a Successful Freight Brokerage Company

By: Doug Yimmer

Table of Contents

Introduction

Transportation is the largest segment of the global economy, with freight-related activities accounting for one third of all global economic activity. It is also one of the most volatile segments of the economy, affected by factors such as changes in fuel costs or new legislation.

The freight broker industry may have gotten its start to move cargo across town but has grown into a multi-billion-dollar industry with more than 20,000 brokers working in most major cities around the world.

Freight brokers play an important role in helping companies move their goods and services from point A to point B. They are essentially middlemen between shippers and carriers who bid on shipments and help arrange delivery. They are paid by the shippers and rely on the carriers to carry out their orders. Carriers, in turn, pay brokers for arranging shipments.

This book, Freight Broker Business: How to Start a Successful Freight Brokerage Company, is written for people interested in learning more about this business. It aims to provide readers with a clear understanding of the freight broker industry and how it works.

Some of the topics discussed in this book include:

- The global transport industry and the role of freight brokers in it.
- The history and evolution of the freight broker industry.
- Freight brokers and their role in helping companies move their goods from point A to point B.
- The global market for freight brokerage services, including information on its size, participants, and future prospects.
- How freight brokers work with shippers and carriers.
- The various activities of freight brokers, including booking, transportation, communications, and payment.
- Freight forwarders vs. brokers; what they do and the services they offer to their clients.
- The business model of a freight broker business.
- How to start a successful freight brokerage company.
- How to build a business plan, including the building blocks of a business plan.
- How to choose the right location for your business.
- The role of the Internet in business and its importance to the freight broker industry.

- Freight broker software and how it can help you start your brokerage company on a strong footing.

At the end of this book, you will be able to make a well-informed decision about whether starting your own freight broker company is right for you.

This book is written for both established and aspiring freight brokers. If you are an aspiring freight broker, you will find it helpful to read this book to understand the industry better and get a sense of what it takes to run such a business.

As the saying goes "knowledge is power." This book aims to provide you with the knowledge necessary to start your own freight broker business and make it a success.
Let's begin.

Chapter 1: The Freight Broker Business and Economy

The freight brokerage business is a very lucrative industry. It can also be very risky. What makes this industry such a financial risk is the fact that it is based on human interaction.

Many people will start up a freight brokerage company and then realize that they have made a mistake. The fact is that you can make an average of $70,000[1] per year in profit if you are doing everything right. On the other hand, you can also lose as much money as if you were to work as an employee and only make minimum wage.

A lot of people have great aspirations for their freight broker business and they want to see it succeed, but when push comes to shove, they fail miserably because of some common mistakes they have made along the way.

In this chapter, we will discuss some of those mistakes and how you can avoid them in order to start up your own

---

[1] Kevin Hill (updated July 29th 2020) https://sonar.freightwaves.com/freight-market-blog/how-do-freight-brokers-get-paid

successful freight brokerage company. We will also discuss the economic environment in which the freight brokerage industry exists.

History of the Freight Broker Industry

During the second half of the 19th century, there was a lot of growth in the railroad industry. Industrialization was in full swing and it was seen that railroads were extremely valuable to the economy. At this time, new laws and regulations were enacted by the government to control railroads. The Interstate Commerce Act and its amendments were passed by Congress in 1887.[2] This act gave the ICC (Interstate Commerce Commission) authority over railroads. The ICC had power to regulate rates, set safety standards, set rules on how much track a railroad could own, etc.

The railroad companies were concerned about the new laws being enacted by Congress because they feared that these rules would cripple their profits and make it impossible for them to run their businesses efficiently. These companies complained to Congress and demanded that they be given some sort of

---

2 United States Senate
https://www.senate.gov/artandhistory/history/minute/Interstate_Commerce_Act_Is_Passed.htm

protection from these new laws. Congress responded with an amendment proposed by Senator John Sherman (R-OH) on August 14, 1887.

The amendment stated that persons who transported property for compensation or hired employees needed a license from the government for this purpose. It also said that no person could perform these activities without a license unless specifically exempted under certain circumstances like intrastate transportation of goods (within one state), transportation of perishable goods, etc. This amendment was passed as part of the Interstate Commerce Act and became law on February 4, 1888.

The railroad industry was satisfied with the amendment and it seemed to fulfill their demands for protection from government regulations. However, this amendment went beyond what was originally intended. It did not just apply to railroads but to anyone who transported anything for compensation other than passengers or their own personal belongings. The amendment covered everything from water carriers to stagecoaches to horse-drawn wagons and all other types of transportation except for those exempted under certain circumstances.

The result was that a lot of small companies suddenly found themselves in violation of the law and faced huge fines if they didn't get a license from the government to transport items for compensation. Companies that were previously exempt under certain circumstances like intrastate transportation had no choice but to obtain a license or be fined by the government. Even though this license was very cheap earlier (a lot less than the amount charged by big freight forwarders today), it added up because a lot of companies were now forced to obtain them in order to continue earning money for their businesses.

The result of this change in legislation is that thousands of new companies began to pop up overnight and it became very difficult for existing companies to compete with them. The new companies were called "freight brokers" and they charged less than railroads or shipping companies. The railroad industry was forced to cut their rates in order to compete with these new upstarts. They even offered special reduced rates for shippers who hired the freight brokers instead of themselves. The freight broker industry flourished during the late 19th century as the railroads were forced to give in to these new "underground" operations because they couldn't compete with them. This also happened at a time when there was a lot of growth in the retail business industry, the manufacturing industry, etc. In fact, the freight broker business became so popular that one out of every five businesses in the U.S. was owned by a freight broker around this time period.

The railroads and shipping companies realized that they needed to do something about this if they wanted to protect their profits from being siphoned off by these "underground" operations. They tried various methods over a few years but they were unsuccessful because of one simple reason: when you are dealing with thousands of small companies and hundreds of thousands of individual workers, it is impossible to enforce the law and regulate them all.

The railroads and shipping companies then decided to go through the government for assistance. They went back to Congress and requested a new amendment that would require a license in order for anyone to operate a freight broker business (or any other type of transportation business). The amendment was passed by Congress in 1887 as part of the Interstate Commerce Act. It was called "The Sherman Antitrust Act."

This law, along with its amendments over time, regulated the freight broker industry until 1980 when it was finally repealed by President Carter. From this time period however, the freight broker industry evolved from being a bunch of small underground operations into the huge current $137[3] billion industry with thousands of big corporations and millions of workers involved with it.

In the late 19th century, the freight broker industry was not even considered an industry by itself. It was just a segment of the railroad and shipping industries. During this time, there were no separate organizations that represented these companies. There were also no separate associations for them to join or attend conferences.

As time went on however, there was a lot of growth in the freight broker business and it became a huge industry all by itself. The National Transportation Brokers Association (NTBA[4]) was formed to represent the interests of freight brokers and take care of their problems such as setting standards in the transportation industry, creating uniform standards for paperwork, etc. NTBA is a non-profit organization that functions as a representative body for truckers and freight brokers.

---

3 Industry statistics U.S. https://www.ibisworld.com/industry-statistics/market-size/freight-forwarding-brokerages-agencies-united-states/

4 NTBA https://www.ntba-brokers.com/

In the late '60s and early '70s during President Nixon's term in office, there was a lot of political pressure from many different interest groups (consumers, environmentalists, trucking companies, etc.) to curb freight costs by passing legislation that would regulate these prices. There were many bills introduced in Congress that would have severely hurt the freight broker industry but they were never passed due to severe retaliation from the public.

The late '70s and early '80s saw a lot of layoffs in the freight broker industry and many freight brokers started to rely on their warehouse operations to help them survive during these tough times. The recession in the '80s was especially hard on the freight broker industry because it was very much affected by the recession and a lot of companies were forced to close down because of this.

The freight broker industry recovered from this recession and came back strong when President Reagan was elected into office. He introduced new laws called "Reaganomics"[5] which helped spur economic growth by slashing taxes, reducing government regulations, etc. Reagan also created an environment that allowed businesses to flourish and made it

---

[5] Will Kenton (updated November 22nd 2020) https://www.investopedia.com/terms/r/reaganomics.asp

easier for companies to enter new markets. This allowed the freight broker business to grow rapidly again during his term in office.

The economic boom in the '90s gave rise to even more growth in this business as well as an increase in demand for international trade and international shipping of goods (especially from Asia). Consumers were now demanding better products at cheaper prices than ever before and this created a lot more business for shipping companies all over the world. This boom continued through 2000 until we reached a point where there were too many shipping companies competing with each other for customers.

In the first decade of the 21st century, there was a lot of consolidation in the freight broker industry by companies like DHL[6] and UPS[7] who wanted to expand their operations into Europe and Asia. They bought a lot of small shipping companies to get what they wanted. The boom continued for a while but eventually, it went from boom to bust due to an economic recession.

The freight broker industry has seen ups and downs over its history but it has remained very resilient through all of these

---

[6] DHL https://www.dhl.com/in-en/home.html

[7] UPS https://www.ups.com/in/

changes. It is a very stable business and, even though it is affected by economic recessions, it has always come back stronger than ever. When one segment of this industry is suffering due to a recession or other problems, another segment will be growing and help pick up the slack as new opportunities arise for business owners who are willing to work hard to succeed in this challenging business.

Freight Brokerage Economy

The economy affects every business and it has a direct impact on the freight broker business. The world economy is undergoing a significant change due to various factors. The consumer market is growing in emerging markets like India and China, creating new opportunities for freight broker companies.

Millennials are the new crop of consumers that have spent more than any generation in history. They are also willing to spend more on freight services compared to previous generations. They prefer using online shipping services because shipping helps them save money and time.

A freight brokerage business is not just about the trucking industry, but also involves ocean cargo shipping, air cargo shipping, rail cargo shipping, and courier services, as well as other transportation services. It can be simple or complex depending on the geographical location of the company and the size of demand for various types of products needed by different industries across countries or states.

The freight broker business is also affected by the regulatory and governmental policies and rules. The industry has a diverse clientele from different industries. The trucking industry, especially the owner-operator truck drivers are facing a lot of challenges in terms of their income. The challenges have been created due to the ever-increasing competition in transportation services.

The freight broker business offers opportunities for drivers to earn more without owning a truck or a tractor trailer and they can work independently for different carriers as an independent contractor, or even work with an owner-operator trucking company. Freight brokering is not just limited to the trucking industry; it covers all types of transportation services. A person who wants to start a freight brokerage company needs to understand all aspects of the business and take advantage of its opportunities.

Freight brokers help trucking companies to get loads and secure payments. They act as an intermediary between the shipper and the trucking company. They help get the best rates for freight services, track shipments, and provide information on the supply and demand of various products needed by different industries.

The demand for freight brokerage services is increasing day by day because of the growth in e-commerce industry, increase in online shopping, growth in retail sector, increase in online marketing, etc. Freight brokerage companies need to keep up with the demand for increased services. This is a growing industry that offers opportunities for people who want to start a business without hefty investments. You can start a freight brokerage business with just one truck or with no trucks at all. It is an ideal business model for those who have been looking for an opportunity to start their own business without big investment or risk involved. The cost of starting a freight broker business is almost negligible when compared to other types of businesses like manufacturing or software development. Freight broker businesses are also easy to manage as it involves less stress than other types of businesses like manufacturing or retail.

Freight brokering is an ideal business for someone who wants to be his own boss and decide his own hours of work. It is an ideal business for those who don't want to go through the stress of working under someone else or for those who don't want to get stuck in traffic jams. Freight brokering is a great opportunity for the people who want to travel the world and enjoy their life without having to worry about managing a business. Freight brokering offers opportunities for people looking for an entrepreneurial career in a relatively new industry that has been growing rapidly over the past decade. There are many opportunities in the freight broking industry, but you need some experience to start a successful freight brokerage business. You need to understand everything related to the shipping and trucking industry, including how it works and what are its challenges. You need good knowledge of computer software as well as knowledge of online shopping portals and more. You also need licenses from regulatory authorities where you want to operate your freight broker business from.

Freight Brokering Supply and Demand

If you are in the business of freight brokering, you need to be aware of the supply and demand on the market. The freight market is like any other market with supply and demand. An over-supply of freight brokers on the market can quickly lead to a shortage of customers, which in turn can lead to lower prices for your services.

The best way to minimize this problem is to offer something that sets you apart from your competition. For example, do you offer more than just a broker service? Do you offer in-house transportation services? Do you provide free advice in areas that differ from just brokering? These are all ways to set yourself apart from your competition.

A good knowledge of the freight markets can be very beneficial when it comes to shipping or other related services. This knowledge can help increase profits by:

Offering lower rates for customers who need shipping services now – If demand is high and supply is low, price increases are likely due to increased demand. You want to take advantage of this by offering low rates now when demand is high. This will ensure that your company has steady cash flow from customers who need a service right away, which will keep them coming back when they need shipping services again.

Finding the perfect price – The perfect price is a balance between your costs and your profit. Finding this perfect price can be difficult, but it can pay off in the long run. The best way to find this balance is to know the market and know where you stand within that market.

Let's take a look at an example of how over-supply can affect the market:

If there are five freight brokers that service a specific area and the demand for freight services is not very high, then it is likely that all five will have a hard time getting customers. This means that they will have to compete with each other for customers.

This competition will likely lead to lower prices for the customers and lower rates of profit. This in turn leads to the possibility of more freight brokers entering this market which can lead to a vicious cycle until there are no customers and no freight brokers.

At this point, you cannot compete based on price alone because none of your competitors will sell at a loss in order to gain more business. Therefore, you need to find a way to set your company apart from other freight brokerage companies so that you get more business than your competitors.

Price is not the only factor though. There are many factors that come into play when it comes to the supply and demand of freight brokerage services. The main factor though is price; price has a big effect on supply and demand. If prices go up, then supply will decrease, while demand increases, which causes prices to go up even more due to increased demand.

Other factors include:

Treating customers fairly – Customers want to feel like they are getting a good deal. If you treat your customers fairly, then you will get repeat business. This is a great way to ensure a steady amount of business from customers who will be happy to refer you to their friends and colleagues.

Experience – Having experience in the freight brokerage industry can help increase profits because it means that your company has a better understanding of how the industry works and what is happening on the market; this leads to better decision making on the company's part.

Marketing – Marketing is a great way to get a steady stream of customers who will keep coming back for more. Marketing is also a great way to get repeat customers because you can offer special deals to new customers to get them interested in your services. These special deals can be used by current customers as well. This will help keep your company in the minds of your customers and keep them coming back for more.

Fees and Costs

Fees and costs are a big part of the freight brokerage business. Fees can be charged in two ways—by the shipment or by a percentage of the freight charge. Fees can even be charged using a combination of these two methods.

Most brokers quote fees based on volume shipped. Brokers who charge fees based on volume usually have a minimum volume per shipment that is required to use their services. For example, a broker may require that the shipment be between 1000 and 2000 pounds, or $500 to $1,000 in value. Once this minimum volume is reached, they bill their fee based upon the actual freight charges.

Brokers who charge by percentage usually charge between 13% and 15%.[8] If you are starting your own brokerage business, you will need to decide which method is best for your

---

[8] Kevin Hill https://sonar.freightwaves.com/freight-market-blog/how-do-freight-brokers-get-paid

business model and clients. The method you choose will determine how much profit you make per shipment based on what your fee is and what your actual freight charges are for each shipment.

The competition in this business can be fierce when starting up your business and attracting clients to use your services. Freight brokers who have been in business for some time have an edge over new brokers because they have established relationships with other freight brokers, trucking companies, and shipping agents. They have also established relationships with their clients and have gained trust from them.

The new broker will have to build their reputation from the ground up. This can take a lot of time that an experienced freight broker may not need to invest. The more you can network with other freight brokers, trucking companies, and shipping agents, the easier it will be for you to build your reputation and attract more clients.

Freight Broker Licensing:

Brokers wishing to apply for a freight broker license must apply for the relevant designation credential with the FMSCA[9]

---

[9] FMSCA https://www.fmcsa.dot.gov/registration/broker-registration

through the Unified Registration System. Many states require that a business license be obtained before any type of business activity can be initiated. Check with your local municipality or state government for the requirements in your area.

External Risks and Liabilities

Because the freight brokerage business is so highly specialized and unique, there are numerous risks that every entrepreneur needs to consider before starting his or her own freight brokerage business. The following are some of the most common risks:

1. Liability to third parties

A freight broker is responsible for, and can be held liable for, the actions of its employees, so a freight broker must take care in hiring and supervising its employees. For example, a freight broker who is aware that an employee is habitually driving unsafely might be liable for injuries caused by the employee's unsafe driving. As a result, it is important for employers to exercise reasonable care in hiring and supervising employees and to implement procedures for monitoring and controlling employee behavior.

2. Financial risks

In addition to general business risks such as inadequate cash flow, failure to meet payroll, or defaulting on loans, there are specific financial risks associated with operating a freight brokerage business. These include:

(a) **Cost risk** – Many costs that are not apparent at first glance can significantly affect the profitability of an operation. For example, one small air carrier may charge 15 cents per mile but another carrier may charge only 3 cents per mile, which means that over the long run the first carrier could be much more expensive than the second carrier even though its initial rates seem comparable. Also, most companies add a surcharge for out-of-route shipments which can vary per shipment depending on the size of the truck involved. So before signing any contracts with an air or trucking company it is important to thoroughly research the cost structure and make sure you are getting a good deal.

(b) **Competition** – It is important to recognize that there is always competition in the freight brokerage business, and it is easy for customers to go elsewhere if they are dissatisfied with their service. This competitive threat means that a freight broker must be well-known within the industry and have a reputation for providing high quality service at a reasonable price. In order to achieve this reputation, it makes sense for a broker to work hard to build good relationships with customers.

(c) **Employee theft** – Freight brokers should implement procedures to limit employee theft, such as not allowing employees free access to cash or checks. Also, if possible, all inventories should be tied down or locked up so that employees cannot easily walk off with merchandise without authorization.

3. Credit risks

There are many kinds of credit risks that can affect a freight brokerage business:

(a) **Credit risk** – A freight broker may extend credit to its customers in order for them to buy products, pay bills, or finance operations. If the customers are unable or unwilling to repay their debts as promised, the freight broker will suffer losses. For example, if a customer makes a cash deposit but then does not pay the freight charges, the freight broker suffers a loss.

(b) **Payment risk** – It is important to recognize that customers often fail to pay their freight bills in a timely fashion. Delinquent payments can be very costly, and it is important to have good collection procedures in place. For example, one way to minimize late payment penalties is for the freight broker to give its customers 30 days before charging a penalty for late payment. Also, it is best to collect money due before shipping merchandise out instead of waiting until after it has been shipped. This will allow you to keep control of your merchandise until you are sure you will be paid for it.

(c) **Foreign exchange risk** – One danger many entrepreneurs face when they are starting out in international trade is that their business may be subject to fluctuations in foreign exchange rates which can have a significant impact on their business. For example, suppose that an exporter agrees to sell goods worth $1 million for an amount equal to 1 million Euros at the time he or she enters into the agreement with his or her customer. Now suppose that during the time between entering into the agreement and the time the goods are delivered, the value of the dollar drops by 25%. This means that after the goods are delivered, the exporter will be paid for them in $1 million, which is equivalent to only 750,000 Euros. Because of this risk, it is a good idea to price freight charges in advance so that you know what you will receive for your goods.

4. Business risks

There are also numerous business risks associated with operating a freight brokerage business:

(a) **Market conditions** – The freight brokerage business is a market-driven industry. In other words, your success as a freight broker depends on how well you satisfy customers' needs and wants. If you fail to provide services that customers need or want, they will go elsewhere in order to get what they want. Also, if your prices are too high or too low compared to those of your competitors then customers might go elsewhere for their services. For example, if you have a monopoly on services in an area then you can charge whatever prices you want and still attract customers because there is no other competition around. However, once competition enters into this market then you must lower your prices or risk losing business to competitors.

(b) **Technology** – The freight brokering industry is constantly changing, and new technologies are constantly being introduced. For example, in recent years the Internet has begun to have a major impact on the freight brokering industry. The Internet allows customers to find out information about various companies at their convenience, and it allows companies to advertise their services without having to spend large amounts of money on advertising. However, in order for a company to be successful in this type of business it is very important to have an effective website. A website must be attractive and easy for customers to use, or else they will go elsewhere.

(c) **Industry trends** – Many businesses fail or experience reduced profits because they do not keep up with industry trends and changes. For example, a freight broker who does not keep up with changing technology may lose a great deal of business if his or her customers can find what they need on the Internet instead of from him or her. It is important not only that you become aware of potential changes but that you also adapt your services accordingly so that you are still compatible with your customers' needs.

(d) **Environmental factors** – One environmental factor that freight brokers should consider is whether or not they will be affected by possible changes in regulations, such as those related to the transportation of hazardous materials. A freight broker who does not keep abreast of these regulations may suddenly find that his or her business is no longer viable because he or she is unable to provide the services their customers need.

(e) **Technology obsolescence** – Technology often becomes obsolete very quickly, and it is important for a freight broker to be able to keep up with technological changes in order to stay competitive in the marketplace. For example, many companies are switching from PCs running Windows operating systems to Macintosh machines, and if an entrepreneur decides not to switch then he or she may be left behind by the rest of the industry.

Freight Brokering Trends

While the freight brokering business is not as popular as it once was, new opportunities are available for those who wish to pursue this line of endeavor. The modern world of shipping has changed dramatically, and the changing economy has opened new markets which were previously closed to both producers and consumers. Freight brokers help producers and suppliers of goods find the most economical means of shipping their products to their destination, and they also help consumers find the best rates on shipping goods from one location to another.

The freight brokering business is a very competitive one, and it has become increasingly more difficult to make a profit in this line of work. This is because there are far more freight brokers now than there were when the business began; and these new brokers aren't just competing with each other for clients, but they are also competing with a number of other companies who offer similar services.

Despite the competition that exists between freight brokers, they have historically been able to establish good working relationships with each other because there is always room for more people in this field. Freight brokers do not generally compete with each other for clients, but they do compete with others in order to get better rates from companies who provide them with transportation services.

The economy has affected the entire industry as well, which has made it harder for freelancers to establish themselves as successful businesses. This is because there are far fewer large shipping companies available today than there were at any time during the 20th century. The economy has forced many companies out of business, and very few of these companies were able to survive as independent entities.

The industry may never return to the level it once was, but there are still opportunities for those who wish to pursue a career in freight brokering. If you have a strong work ethic, and you are willing to learn as much as possible about the business, then you can establish yourself as a successful freight broker by completing the necessary training and obtaining the proper licenses.

The Profitability of Freight Brokering

As a freight broker, you can profit from the cost savings of a freight broker business. A freight broker business can save your clients at least 10% to 15%[10] on their transportation costs. This means that if a shipper is currently paying $100,000 per year for transportation, they could potentially be paying $85,000 per year by going through a freight broker firm.

The demand for freight brokers is very high and growing because businesses are looking to cut costs and save money on transportation. Freight brokers are able to offer better rates because they are buying in volume from the carriers and then reselling it to the shipper at lower prices.

A freight broker business is very profitable because you can charge a fee that is a percentage of the cost savings to your clients. For example, if you can save your clients 40% on their

---

[10] Rob Bade https://blog.kencogroup.com/7-ways-your-freight-broker-lowers-transportation-costs

transportation costs, then you could charge a commission rate of 2% on the savings.

The other great thing about this type of business is that it doesn't matter how much your clients spend with you. If they are saving $100,000 per year with a freight broker firm, they are going to pay up to $2,000 for the brokerage service. In most cases though, they are going to be paying much less than this because they will be paying for transportation only when they need it and not all year long.

Freight brokers make anywhere from $50,000 per year up to $500,000 per year depending on how successful their business is and where they live. The top 10% of the freight brokers made more than two billion dollars in 2013[11] and these businesses tend to be located in large metropolitan areas like New York City or Chicago. In general, the annual income for freight brokers is estimated to be an average of $70,000.[12]

The cost of starting a freight broker business is very low. You can start a freight brokerage company for around $4,000-

---

[11] Patrick Burnson https://www.supplychain247.com/article/2013_top_50_global_top_30_domestic_3pls

[12] Kevin Hill https://sonar.freightwaves.com/freight-market-blog/how-do-freight-brokers-get-paid

$5,000[13] in startup costs and you will have everything you need to get started right away. The benefit of this type of business is that you don't need employees or inventory or anything else to get started and this makes it easy to start and grow your business.

---

[13] Start-up costs https://www.jwsuretybonds.com/blog/how-much-does-it-cost-to-become-a-freight-broker

Chapter 2: How to Start a Freight Brokerage Company

Freight brokers operate in commercial and industrial sectors to help companies find the best freight rates and to ensure that shipments arrive on time. Freight brokers work closely with logistics professionals and shipping companies to provide a wide range of services. Freight brokers are needed in nearly every industry, from manufacturing to retailing, from construction to healthcare.

Freight brokers arrange for cargo to be transported between business locations or from one location to another. Freight brokers have access to a variety of transportation modes including airplanes, trucks, ships, trains, and even planes. Most buyers do not have the experience or resources necessary to arrange for shipping on their own. Instead, they rely on freight brokers for help in arranging for shipments.

In this chapter, we will explore the steps you need to follow in order to start a freight brokerage company. Let's get started.

Freight Broker Services

Freight broker services are designed to be an intermediary between shipper and truck driver. A freight broker is a transporter who arranges the transportation of freight from one location to another. The freight transportation is arranged by brokers/agents on behalf of the shippers. Freight brokers work with trucking companies, railroads, shipping lines, warehouses, and other transporters to arrange the transportation of cargo in freight trucks or ships or both. If you are looking for freight broker services, then you have come to the right place as we provide quality services in this regard.

Freight broker services are of two types in North America:

Load board services:

In this type of service, the freight brokers advertise their service on a load board or computer that lists all available truckload capacity for a given period. Shippers can make direct contact with brokers to arrange transport services. No commission is charged by the load board.

Commission based services:

In this type of service, the brokers earn commission from the carriers for each load arranged. Freight brokers software is used to facilitate this method of operations. The broker gets paid by the shipper and then pays the carrier via check or direct deposit.

Carrier Consolidation Services

This type of service facilitates consolidation of loads to reduce transportation costs. The freight broker assists shippers to consolidate freight loads into one shipment in order to reduce transportation costs by reducing fuel consumption and saving time for drivers. Freight broker services are an integral part of the logistics industry as all businesses need good logistics support for their business operations to run smoothly and profitably.

Freight brokerage services are provided by logistics companies as well as freight brokers associations throughout the United States and Canada. Freight brokerage companies offer many kinds of special services including environmentally friendly shipping, high value shipments, legal shipments, dangerous goods shipping, out of gauge shipments, and many other services. Freight brokers can help clients to identify the right transportation solution for their goods and products. In addition to transportation services, freight brokers act as a medium of communication between the clients and the transport agency, thereby ensuring safe delivery and pickup of the goods.

Here are the different services offered by a licensed freight broker:

1. Air Freight Forwarding Services

Air freight forwarding services are provided by freight brokers to air freight cargo due to its better handling and safe delivery. Air freight forwarding services are designed to facilitate the movement of goods via air cargo. Air freight services are required for transportation of goods that have to be transported very quickly while ensuring maximum safety requirements.

2. Ocean Freight Services

Ocean freight forwarding services are designed to facilitate the transportation of goods by sea cargo. Ocean freight services are required for transporting goods that are too big or too heavy to be transported by road and air. Ocean freight services are provided by freighters which carry cargo on a regular schedule between different ports.

3. Customs Broker Services

Customs broker services offer a wide range of customs brokerage services to help clients with all their customs needs from pre-arrival filing and clearance through delivery. Customs broker services can be easily accessed over the Internet for trade compliance and import/export consulting, processing, documentation preparation, examination and negotiation of duties, fees, taxes, and penalties. Many customs brokers provide full service including preparation of documentation, filing for permits, post entry audit support, as well as clearance and delivery of cargo in port cities throughout the United States and Canada as well as worldwide ports such as Singapore, Hong Kong, Taiwan, etc.

4. LCL (Less than Container Load) Shipping Services

LCL shipping services are provided by freight brokers to facilitate transportation of goods which cannot be placed in a container such as automobiles or machines that are too big or heavy to be transported in containers. LCL shipping services are provided by ocean transport vessels that carry cargo on a regular schedule between different ports.

5. Heavy Haul Transportation Services

Heavy haul transportation services are required for transportation of heavy equipment, construction materials, and machinery. These services are very important for the movement of heavy loads that cannot be placed in a container and need to be transported by road. These services are provided by freight brokers who also offer other freight transportation solutions such as trucking, rail freight, air freight, and ocean shipping. Heavy haul transportation services can be very expensive as they require special equipment such as trucking cranes in order to load the cargo on trucks or ships from manufacturing centers or warehouses to ports, or from the ports to the customers' locations.

6. Bulk Shipping Services

Bulk shipping services are required for transporting goods that cannot be placed in a container such as sand, gravel, and raw materials when they are shipped from manufacturing plants directly to construction sites in their original form without processing or blending with other substances. Bulk shipping is generally provided by specialized ships such as bulk carriers which carry cargo on a regular schedule between different ports while transporting only one type of cargo at a time using special procedures designed to maintain its quality.

7. Heavy Lift Transportation Services

Heavy lift transportation services are required for transporting heavy equipment and machinery that cannot be placed in a container. These services can be provided by freight brokers who can also offer other freight transportation solutions such as trucking, rail freight, air freight, and ocean shipping. Heavy lift services are provided by specialized vessels such as heavy cargo ships which carry cargo on a regular schedule between different ports while transporting only one type of cargo at a time using special procedures designed to maintain its quality.

8. Trucking Services

Trucking services are provided for the transportation of goods in trucks from one location to another. Freight brokers can help shippers and consignees to find trucking companies that best suit their needs based on price, service level, deadlines, and other important criteria such as environmental friendliness, hours of operations, and so on. Freight brokers can also assist shippers and consignees to negotiate with trucking companies for the best rates based on their needs, whether it is a one-time shipment or regular shipments throughout the United States or Canada or even worldwide through our international logistics network. In addition, freight brokers provide customs broker services for import and export shipments via truck as well as via other modes of transportation such as sea freight, air freight, rail freight, and ocean shipping.

Company Business Plan

The first thing you need to do is to decide your niche type. You can either choose the freight forwarding type or the auctioning type. I will recommend you to choose the auctioning type because this method is more profitable and easier to operate than the forwarding type.

Let's take a look at what you need in your business plan:

1. Company Profile

The company profile is the most important part in your business plan. In this section, you need to introduce your company and the market in which you are going to operate. You also need to write down the strategy of your business, such as how you are going to attract clients and what is your unique selling point.

For example, you can write about your company:

- The owner's experience in the shipping industry and his/her vision for this industry.

- The company's mission statement and its vision of the future.
- The company's goals for the next five years.
- The company's key values, such as honesty, fairness, and integrity.

2. Management Team & Staff Profile

In this section, you need to write down the education background of your management team and staff. You also need to describe their work experience in this field and their strengths and weaknesses. Furthermore, you need to write about each staff's job description and his/her responsibilities.

For example, you can write:

- The CEO's education background and his/her years of experience in the shipping industry. You also need to describe his/her strengths and weaknesses.
- The CFO's education background, years of experience, and strengths and weaknesses.
- The COO's education background, years of experience, and strengths and weaknesses.

3. Company Strategy & Business Plan

In this section, you need to introduce your business strategy, such as how you are going to reach your goals, what is the company's unique selling point, and what is your marketing plan. You also need to explain the company culture, its financial plan for next year, and how you are going to operate in the future.

For example, you can write about your strategy:

- The company's goals for the next five years.
- The company's key values, such as honesty, fairness, and integrity.
- How you are going to reach your goals. For example, you can write about your marketing plan and how you are going to attract clients.

4. Company Financial Plan & Ratios Analysis

In this section, you need to write about the amount of money required to start your business and what is the total amount of money that you need five years from now. You also need to write down how much money will be generated from each department and how much profit the company makes each month. Furthermore, you need to analyze different ratios of your business to see if it is profitable.

For example:
"Our company will be profitable in the first year because we are going to start with $1,000,000. The total amount of money needed in five years is $1,500,000. We will make $250,000 each month from department X. We will need $120,000 to buy a new truck in two years. Each month, our company will make $41,250 profit."

5. Industry Analysis

In this section, you need to write about your competition. You also need to write about the market and its trend in the next five years. You also need to write down the market share for your company and its competitors. Furthermore, you need to write about your company's competitive advantage and what makes your company different from your competitors.

For example, you can write about the market:
"Our industry is profitable because there is a high demand for this service. Our company will make $1,500,000 in annual revenue because we have a competitive advantage over our competitors."

6. SWOT Analysis

A SWOT Analysis contains four elements: Strength, Weaknesses, Opportunities, and Threats. In this section, you need to write down your company's strengths and weaknesses. You also need to write about opportunities and threats that are related to your business. Furthermore, you need to analyze how opportunities and threats are related to each other and how they affect your business. The final piece is to write down recommendations for improving your business.

For example:
"Our company's strengths are its competitive advantage over our competitors. The threats are the changes that will happen in the shipping industry."

7. Competitor Analysis

You need to write about your competitors and their strengths and weaknesses. You also need to write about the changes that are happening in the shipping industry and how these changes affect your business. Furthermore, you need to analyze how your company is different from your competitors and how it can attract more clients.

For example:
"Our competitors have a lower price than ours. They are also less efficient than us because they don't have our unique selling point."

Startup Costs

There are a few different ways to start a freight brokerage business, and the costs will vary depending on how you want your company to operate. Some startups will require more startup capital than others, but it's important to take a look at what type of freight broker business you want to run.

If you want to run an honest and trustworthy business, your startup costs will be much higher. You'll need to purchase several different types of insurance policies, including workers' compensation, liability insurance, automobile insurance, and more.

You'll also need a business bank account and a business credit card to handle all of the payments you receive from your customers. These costs are required by state law, so if you fail to purchase them, your freight brokerage company could be shut down.

In order to start a freight brokerage company, you'll need to purchase any licenses or permits you'll need. You may need to obtain a license in order to broker freight and transport products for your customers. If you don't have a license, you could be shut down by the state or federal government.

You'll also need software programs in order to run your business efficiently and effectively. There are several different software programs that can help you keep track of payments and shipments, and they're fairly affordable for new startups. The costs depend on the type of software that you choose to use.

Here is the breakdown of the average startup costs:

1. Business registration - $100 to $300
2. Business surety bond - $900 to $9,000
3. Software programs - $100 to $1,000

The total startup costs of a freight brokerage business:

The average startup costs of a freight brokerage company are around $10,000.[14] However, if you plan on running an honest and trustworthy business with high standards, your startup

---

[14] Freight broker costs https://www.bryantsuretybonds.com/blog/cost-freight-broker

costs will be higher. The more money you spend on your business at the beginning, the better off you'll be in the long run.

As far as software programs go, there are several different options available that can help you run your business more effectively and efficiently. There are many different types of software programs available on the market today, so it's important to take a look at each one before making your final decision. The software is affordable for most startups, but you should make sure it's going to help you run your company properly before purchasing it.

Freight Broker Marketing Strategy

Your marketing strategies will determine the success of your freight brokerage company. A freight broker marketing strategy is a plan that outlines the different approaches you should take to reach your target audience.

A freight broker marketing strategy includes the following:

Marketing strategy – How you will present your company and the mediums you will use to promote your business are part of a freight broker marketing strategy. You can use a variety of different marketing strategies to promote your business including online ads, newspaper ads, radio commercials, etc. The main point of a freight broker marketing strategy is to reach as many people as possible in order to generate more leads for your business.

Target audience – Before developing a freight broker marketing strategy, it's important to define who your target market is (the people you want to do business with). You may want to focus on serving retailers or manufacturers or both. It's important that you select an audience that fits well with the services you provide and one that will help you grow your business.

Competition – Although there are many businesses involved in the transportation industry, there is still a lot of room for growth in this area and more opportunities for success. However, when deciding on a target audience and developing a freight broker marketing strategy, it's also important to consider the competition that you'll face. If you're entering a market where there is already a lot of competition, it's important to come up with a unique selling point (USP) that will set you apart from the competition.

Promotion – Freight broker marketing strategy also includes promotion. A freight broker marketing strategy should include different ways to promote your company including online ads, newspaper ads, radio commercials, etc. The main point of a marketing strategy is to reach as many people as possible in order to generate more leads for your business.

Here are some of the top freight broker marketing channels:

Print advertising – Print advertising includes newspapers, magazines, yellow pages, etc. It's an effective way to reach your target audience since it's a medium that most people check regularly. However, print advertising can be expensive and there is a lot of competition.

For example, if you want to run a newspaper ad, you'll have to pay the newspaper in advance for a certain number of ad spaces. This can be expensive and you'll also need to compete with other local businesses that are running ads in the same newspaper.

Radio advertising – Radio ads are another effective way to reach your target audience since many people listen to the radio every day. However, radio ads are also expensive and there is a lot of competition for radio airtime.

An example of how radio advertising is used is by running a commercial during a popular radio show. This is an effective way to reach your target market since people are listening to the same radio station and might hear your ad. However, if you're not careful, you might end up paying a lot of money for airtime that nobody will ever hear.

Online ads – Online ads are another effective way to reach your target audience since many people use the Internet every day. Online ads can be placed on websites that have large amounts of traffic and can be targeted based on specific keywords. However, online ads are also expensive and there is a lot of competition for ad space.

For example, if you want to run an online ad, you'll have to pay the website in advance for a certain number of ad spaces. This can be expensive and you'll also need to compete with other local or even global businesses that are running ads on the same website.

A good example is to use Google AdWords. If you're not familiar with it, Google AdWords allows you to place text ads on the Google search results page. Google AdWords is a great way to reach your target market because it's an extremely popular website that has a lot of traffic. However, it's also very expensive and there is a lot of competition for ad space on the Google search results page.

Direct mail – Direct mail includes sending mail or postcards directly to potential leads in order to promote your business. It's an effective way to reach your target audience since it's inexpensive and can be effective if used correctly. However, direct mail can be very expensive in bulk and there is a lot of competition for postal addresses.

For example, if you want to send a direct mail piece to potential leads, you'll have to pay the postal service in advance for postage. This can be expensive and you'll also need to compete with other local businesses that are sending mailers to the same postal addresses.

Web – The Internet is a popular way to reach your target audience since it's very versatile and can reach people all over the world. However, Internet marketing can also be very expensive and there is a lot of competition for online ad space. There are many different websites that you can use including search engines like Google or Yahoo! or even social media sites like Facebook and Twitter. There are also many different formats that you can use including banners, videos, infographics, etc.

For example, one popular way to promote your freight broker business online is by creating an account on Facebook and posting ads or updates on your company's pages. This is very effective because it allows followers from all over the world to see your updates regardless if they're in your city or not. However, advertising on Facebook can be expensive and there is a lot of competition for ad space on Facebook pages.

Each freight broker marketing channel has its benefits and drawbacks. It's important to be aware of these benefits and drawbacks before deciding on which freight broker marketing channels you want to use. You may also find it beneficial to use a combination of freight broker marketing channels in order to reach your target audience. For example, you can use newspaper ads and radio commercials at the same time in order to reach people in multiple ways.

Freight Broker Market Research:

Market research is the process of discovering information about your target audience and competition. It's a critical part of any freight broker business plan because it will help you determine if there is enough demand for your product or service in the market and if there is enough room for growth for your business. Your market research should include:

Population – The first thing that you'll need to do when doing market research is determine how many people live in your city or state. This will help you determine how large the potential market is that you have available to reach with your business. Population statistics are usually available through government websites like www.census.gov or www.censusfinder.com.

Number of businesses – Once you know how many people live in your city, you can determine how many businesses are in your city. This will help you determine how much competition exists for your business and give you an idea of how much potential growth there is for your business.

Types of businesses – It's important to also look at the types of businesses that exist in your market since this can help you determine if there is a need for a new type of service in the market or if there is already a lot of competition for what you're offering. If you have identified a type of service that doesn't already exist in the market and there is enough demand, this could be an opportunity to create a new freight broker company.

Example: You may decide to create a new freight broker company that specializes in shipping furniture since it's something that doesn't already exist in the market and there are many potential customers with large shipments of furniture. However, if after doing some research on the types of businesses that exist in your market, you discover that most furniture companies already offer shipping services and do it themselves, this may not be an opportunity to start a freight broker business.

Consumers – Another aspect of market research is determining who the consumers are in your market and what they're looking for. You can do this by doing some online research on local business organizations like Chambers of Commerce or small business organizations that offer networking events for local business owners. You can also do this by speaking to people directly in these organizations or by conducting surveys.

Competitive analysis – The final part of any freight broker market research should include a competitive analysis. This involves identifying the main competitors in your market and comparing their strengths and weaknesses against your own strengths and weaknesses. It's similar to a SWOT (strengths, weaknesses, opportunities, threats) analysis and should be done when developing a freight broker business plan since it will help you determine if there is enough room for growth for your company in the market.

Freight Broker Software

Freight broker software is a program used by freight brokers to automate the entire freight brokering process. It can be either purchased as a stand-alone application or as an integrated part of a freight management software package. The first step to success in this industry is to get organized with an excellent and powerful freight broker software package. Some popular freight broker software programs are:

Exact Freight – Freight management software for freight brokers and trucking companies. This is one of the most powerful freight management software packages on the market today with over 150 modules available including accounts receivable, accounts payable, inventory control, and more.

TMS – Advanced freight management software for trucking companies. It includes complete accounting, dispatch, and logistics capabilities that allow you to manage your complete business using one program.

Global Dispatch – Complete dispatching system for trucking companies and rail carriers with integrated shipping capabilities.

Freight Manager – Complete system for managing your entire business including accounts receivable, accounts payable, inventory control, carrier information, job costing, rate calculations, and more!

Freight Broker Software – These are the most popular freight management software packages that are available for purchase today. They can be purchased as stand-alone applications or integrated into a complete logistics management program.

Using the right software will make all the difference in the world when it comes to success as a freight broker.

Freight Broker Equipment

The equipment needed to run a freight broker business is minimal. Freight brokers are not required to have an office, although they may prefer to work from an office space. Freight brokers should have a computer with Internet access, a fax machine, and a cell phone. The freight broker will need to have accounts with the major freight companies such as UPS and

FedEx[15] and the freight forwarding companies such as Kuehne + Nagel[16] and DHL Global Forwarding.

Here are some of the equipment that a freight broker may use.

Cell phone – A cell phone is needed to contact the freight companies and the shippers. Some cell phones have a feature that allows you to enter a tracking number and obtain the current status of a shipment. This helps the freight broker follow up on shipments that are behind schedule or need to be tracked down.

Computer – A computer with Internet access is needed to search for rates, obtain rate quotes, and generate invoices. Many freight forwarders, such as Kuehne + Nagel, allow their clients to view rates online. This allows a freight forwarder to obtain rates in advance of calling an agent or broker.

Printer/Fax Machine – A printer is used to print shipping labels, invoices, bills of lading, and packing slips. A fax machine is used for sending documents electronically and for receiving documents from customers and other brokers. The fax machine can also be used to contact the freight companies

---

15 FedEx https://www.fedex.com/

16 Kuehne + Nagel https://kuehne-nagel.com/

when having difficulty obtaining information by telephone or when making changes to a shipment's routing instructions.

If you are starting a freight brokerage company, you may want to obtain a dedicated fax line that is not shared by other users in your office. Faxes are used constantly and a dedicated line will allow you to print shipping labels without having to wait for the other users in your office to finish printing their documents.

Shipping Scale – A shipping scale is needed to weigh shipments of hazardous materials or heavy items such as machinery. A shipping scale is also required when shipping air freight.

Freight Broker Networking

Networking is a vital part of the freight brokerage business. The key to successful networking is being prepared and knowing what to talk about. You definitely don't want to spend your time talking about the weather or what happened on the local news. If you do that, you will come across as a shallow individual and your chances of doing business with a client will diminish greatly.

Preparing for Networking Events:

Prepare a brief brokering presentation for handing out to clients and potential clients. When I say brief, I mean brief. Remember, everyone in attendance that evening has other things they need to be doing besides listening to you ramble on about your freight company for an hour. If you can keep it under five minutes, then do so.

Focus on key points of your freight brokerage company that would be of interest to others such as:

> 1) What type of freight are you brokering? (i.e., OTR, LTL, Intermodal)
> 2) Volume of freight handled by month/year, average per month/year? (if it's not much then don't tell them - everyone has low volume)
> 3) How long have you been in business and what type of freight experience do you have?
> 4) What type of freight brokers do you deal with? (i.e., LTL, OTR, Intermodal)
> 5) Do you deal with the trucking companies directly or third-party brokers? (most important question to ask—if they answer third party brokers then skip them

and move on to the next person in line—don't waste your time)

6) How do customers get in touch with you? (tell them how and when they can reach you)

7) Other services offered by your brokerage company. (i.e., warehouse, office space, etc.)

8) Your contact information. (i.e., cell, email address, and/or phone number.) Give them all of it so we can try to reach out to them after the event is over. If we don't get a chance to meet with them at the event then we will pass along our information for follow up at a later time. If they give us their email address then be sure to follow up with a brief email the next day thanking them for their time and inquiring about future business opportunities together.

Speaking Your Mind: Don't be afraid to speak your mind about industry trends or issues that you feel are important to you and your business. It's a networking event so people will be more open to discussing business issues with you.

Questions to Ask Your Networking Partners: If someone hands you a brochure or business card, take a moment and read it over before thanking them for their time. Then turn the conversation into a question-and-answer session as follows: "I see that you are XYZ Company. How long have you been in business?" Let them take the lead from there and ask any other questions that are on their mind. They will be impressed with your knowledge of the freight brokerage business and hopefully they will remember talking with you at the event and follow up with future opportunities for business via email, phone call, or even an invitation to stop by their office for a visit sometime soon.

The Challenge: Don't just focus on networking with people directly at your event. Be sure to network with anyone else who is there even if they are not in the freight brokerage industry, but know someone in the industry. You never know where those connections can lead down the road when needed for future opportunities for profitable freight brokerage business deals.

Chapter 3: The Stakeholders of a Freight Brokerage Company

A freight broker is the person or company which helps the customers to find and select the best service providers for their freight cargo or transport. It is just like a middleman between the customers and service providers. Sometimes they also help in arranging custom clearance, help in successful delivery of the customer's freight, and many more services. There are several companies involved in this business, so it can be difficult for you to get the required service. Therefore, you should have a perfect knowledge about this business before starting it.

Knowing who the stakeholders of a freight brokerage company are is very important before starting the business. Without a clear idea on this, it would be very difficult for you to run a successful business. Let us have a look at the stakeholders in this chapter.

Freight Brokerage Company Stakeholder's Overview

There are several stakeholders of a freight brokerage company. If you want to understand this business properly, then you must have a clear knowledge on them.

A customer is the very first and foremost stakeholder of the freight brokerage company. The customers will be the one who will provide you with the business, so they are an important person in this. You need to do whatever it takes to satisfy your customers. Otherwise, they will not come back to you again.

Another very important stakeholder of a freight brokerage company is your employees. They are the ones who will help you in running this business efficiently and help you in increasing your revenue and profit. Without them, it would be difficult for you to run a successful business. Therefore, always treat them well and pay them well so that they work hard for your business and give their best performance every day.

You should have a strong relationship with all your vendors as well as suppliers as they can easily provide you with high quality products at lower prices than any other person or company can do for you. If they are not happy with you, it will be very difficult for you to run your business smoothly which would result in loss of time and money for the business owner. Therefore, you should always maintain a strong relationship with them.

The last but not the least important stakeholder of a freight brokerage company is your banker. A good relationship with him will help you in getting loans at lower interest rates, which will help you in increasing your profit. Therefore, before starting your business venture, you should have a clear knowledge about this stakeholder and manage your relationships well with them.

Following are the important stakeholders of a freight brokerage company:

1. Customers:

This is by far the most important stakeholder of the freight brokerage company. Customers are the ultimate source of all revenue in the freight brokerage business. Without customers, a brokerage firm cannot survive. The customers of a freight brokerage company are generally the freight forwarding companies, customs brokers, shipping lines, and other shippers. The customers can be end users (consumers) or intermediate users (wholesalers and retailers) of the shipped products.

2. Freight Forwarders:

Freight forwarders are an important customer segment for a freight broker. Freight forwarders are used to receive shipments from exporters on behalf of the actual consignee or importer. In return they charge fees as a percentage of gross invoice value or as a fixed fee per shipment basis. These fees vary depending upon whether it is for import or export shipments, specific types of goods being shipped, size and weight of shipment, value, etc. When they receive shipments on behalf of their clients, they have to pay carriage charges to carriers who ship goods on their behalf like airlines, trucking companies, etc., and so they pass these costs to their clients (importers/exporters). For example: If an air freight forwarder receives 30 shipments per month at an average gross invoice value of $100,000 and their charges are 5% of gross invoice value, then they charge $5,000 per shipment. If the air freight forwarder has to pay $1,200 to an air carrier for each shipment, then the air freight forwarder charges the importer/exporter to cover these costs.

3. Customs Brokers:

Customs brokers are another important customer segment for a freight broker. They are used by exporters and importers to clear shipments at port of entry or exit. They charge fees based on the value and type of goods being shipped in addition to government levied duties and taxes. Customs brokers also charge a percentage fee based on gross invoice value of shipments or fixed fees per shipping unit basis. For example: If an importer has five shipments imported into his warehouse from overseas at an average gross invoice value of $20,000 and customs broker charges 3% of gross invoice value plus $100 per shipment, then the customs broker charges the importer $600 ($20,000 x 3%) + $100 = $700 per shipment. On the other hand, if the customs broker charges a fixed fee of $500 per shipment for all shipments, then the importer has to pay $500 for each shipment.

4. Shipping Lines:

Shipping lines are another important customer segment for a freight broker. They provide access to ocean transportation service on their vessels to shippers/consignees who either have cargo on board or wish to ship goods on board a vessel. Shipping lines charge freight rates based upon several factors like size and weight of shipment or distance covered by the vessel. When shipping lines transport goods onto their vessels they have to pay charges like port charges, pilotage charges, etc., which are passed on to shippers/consignees by shipping lines in the form of freight rates. For example: If an importer has five shipments imported into his warehouse from overseas at an average gross invoice value of $20,000 and shipping line charges 1% of gross invoice value plus $100 per shipment, then shipping line charges the importer $200 ($20,000 x 1%) + $100 = $300 x 5 = $1,500. On the other hand, if a shipping line charges a fixed fee of $500 per shipment for all shipments, then the importer has to pay $2500 total for five shipments.

5. Shippers/Consignees:

Shippers/consignees are another important customer segment for a freight broker. Generally, shippers/consignees are the final users of imported or exported goods and they include consumers, wholesalers, and retailers. Shippers/consignees normally ship goods by paying the shipping line directly. However, in some cases they may use the services of freight forwarders or customs brokers to clear their shipments at port of entry or exit on their behalf. When they use the services of a freight forwarder or customs broker, they have to pay brokerage fees as mentioned above to cover charges levied by these service providers. For example: If an importer has five shipments imported into his warehouse from overseas at an average gross invoice value of $10,000 and shipping line charges 1% of gross invoice value plus $100 per shipment, then the shipping line charges the importer $200 for each shipment. On the other hand, if a shipping line charges a fixed fee of $500 per shipment for all shipments, then the importer has to pay $500 for each shipment.

6. Bankers:

As discussed earlier, bank financing is a very important source of funding for the freight brokerage business. Most freight brokerage firms require institutional funding from banks for their business operations. For example: If a freight brokerage firm has $500,000 worth of annual working capital requirement and has a net worth of $50,000, then it will need to have $450,000 ($500,000 - $50,000) funded by banks through loans and/or lines of credit.

7. Transport Providers:

Transport providers are another important stakeholder of freight brokerage business because they provide access to transportation services to shippers/consignees who have goods to be shipped or wish to ship goods by paying carriage charges for shipping services obtained from them. Carriage charges would include payments made against transportation services like air freight rates (airport-airport), ocean freights (port-port), etc.

8. Regulators:

Regulators are another important stakeholder of freight brokerage business because they regulate the activities of freight brokers and other logistics service providers. Regulators would include government agencies like Federal Maritime Commission (FMC) and Federal Aviation Administration (FAA) in USA; Office of the Fair Trade (OFT) in UK; Canada Industrial Transportation Association (CITA) and Canadian National Transportation Agency in Canada; Department of Transport (DOT), Public Utilities Commission (PUC), etc. in USA; and CAAI in India to name a few.

Shippers and Their Role in a Freight Brokerage Company

Shippers are the ultimate clients of a freight brokerage company because they are the customers. These shippers have no direct interaction with the transport companies. They deal directly with a freight broker company and don't interact with transport companies directly. The shipper is a person who wants to ship his goods from one location to another location.

How you work with shippers:

First, you need to visit the shipper's office or residence. Then you must know their goods' movement needs. You should find out what kind of goods they are shipping, how frequently they need to ship the goods, and where these goods are going.

You can collect the information about shippers through two ways:

The first way is visiting the shippers. This is a good way to get to know your shippers. But it's not effective all the time because some shippers don't have enough time for you or are very busy in their daily routines. Busy shippers will prefer the second option of connecting—that is giving them a call and talking about their needs over the phone.

Your responsibility to the shippers as a freight brokerage company:

First, you need to communicate with your shipper regularly to know about his shipment needs.

You should keep your shipper informed about the appropriate car transport companies that you have selected for him and also let him know if there will be any changes from your side regarding his shipment. If there will be any changes regarding his shipment, let him know immediately. Also keep the shipper informed about the status of his shipment at regular intervals.

Why are shippers so important to your freight brokerage company?

As I have discussed above, you need to communicate with your shippers regularly so that they can get the best service from you and they can be aware of their shipments' status. If they get good service from you then they will surely come to you again and again when they need to ship their goods in the future. So, it's necessary for your freight brokerage company that your shippers are happy with you and get great service from you at all times. Repeat business is one of the main reasons why shippers are so important to a freight brokerage company. So, you should always try to give them the best services.

Role of Freight Agents in a Freight Brokerage Company

Freight agents are the people who work for a freight brokerage company and they have direct interaction with transport companies.

How you work with freight agents:

In a freight brokerage company, freight agents deal directly with transport companies. They have no direct interaction with shippers. They just communicate with transport companies regarding their shipment requirements and they can also negotiate deals on behalf of their clients, i.e., shippers.

How to find freight agents:

Finding a freight agent is not a big deal because some of your friends or relatives can be your first freight agent or you can find any local person to be your first freight agent.

But finding an effective freight agent is very important for your business because your business will not grow if you hire an ineffective freight agent. An ineffective freight agent will get you less business from transport companies and will not be able to satisfy customers, so they will go to another freight broker company where they will get better services. So it's very important to find an effective freight agent for your business.

You can replace your ineffective freight agent with another one in the future, but it will be a huge problem for your business because you will lose all your customers and you will have to start again from the beginning. So, always try to find an effective freight agent for your freight brokerage company so that you can get more business from car transport companies in the future and also satisfy all your shippers.

Freight agents' responsibility to your freight brokerage company:

First, they should know about the requirements of the shipper. Then they should communicate with transport companies regarding their shipment requirements and negotiate a deal on behalf of their clients, i.e., shippers. They should collect all the information about transport companies and let them know about their clients' requirements so that they can provide them with the best services.

They should communicate with transport companies about any changes regarding shipments of their clients immediately so that transport companies can take necessary action if they need to do anything like change the driver or change the vehicle.

Given that most of them operate virtually, they can only communicate with transport companies through emails or phone calls only. They keep their clients informed about the status of their shipments at regular intervals.

Role of Freight Forwarders in a Freight Brokerage Company

Freight forwarders are also one of the stakeholders of a freight brokerage company. Freight forwarders are the people who work as intermediaries between a shipper and a transport company. These freight forwarders manage all the paperwork between shippers and transport companies. They work as an agent between shippers and transport companies.

How you work with freight forwarders:

You should first contact freight forwarders in your area. Then you should ask about the services that they provide to their clients. You should also learn about the procedures they follow while shipping any goods from one location to another location.

You can collect the information about freight forwarders through two ways:

The first way is visiting them at their office or residence or both places if available. This is one good way to get more info from them but it's not effective all the time because they may be very busy and unavailable to during their daily work routines. An alternative option is to give them a call and discuss their services over the phone.

You should communicate with your freight forwarder regularly to let him know about your services that you provide to your clients.

Freight forwarders' responsibility to your freight brokerage company:

Freight forwarders are the agents of your freight brokerage company. They will communicate with your clients on behalf of your freight brokerage company. They will provide full support to your clients in shipping their goods from one location to another location.

Your responsibility to your freight forwarders:

You should also provide full support to your freight forwarders by providing them with all the information that they need regarding your services. You should also provide them with the contact information of your clients so that they can contact them and send their clients to you for shipping their goods from one location to another location.

How freight forwarders work with you:

Freight forwarders in the USA are getting more profit through working with freight brokers because their income is increasing day by day. Freight forwarders contact freight brokers if any of their clients need someone who provides transport services to move their goods from one location to another location. If they are not able to find any transport service providers, then they contact different transport companies directly and ask them for booking orders. When the booking orders are done then the freight forwarder will contact the freight broker and inform him of the booking order number. If a transport company accepts that booking order then the freight forwarder will contact his client and will ask him or her for the shipment details: where he wants his shipment to go, what kind of shipment it is, i.e., package, car, truck, industrial goods, etc.

Regulators of the Freight Brokerage Company

Freight brokerage companies, in general, are subject to the same laws and regulations as other insurance companies. Among them are the Federal Trade Commission, the Bureau of Consumer Protection, the Department of Insurance, and the Office of the Attorney General.

The state laws have a direct effect on how freight brokers operate in their jurisdictions. The licensing requirements for freight brokerage companies vary from state to state with some states having no specific licensing scheme for freight brokers at all.

Some states have different licensing schemes for small and large firms. Many states do not license brokers by their size but only regulate them depending on whether they deal with household goods or commercial property. States that do not license by size usually require a broker to maintain a minimum financial net worth depending on the volume of business conducted by the company in the preceding year. Other states simply treat all freight brokerages as if they were short-term insurers thereby requiring them to obtain a license under an applicable short-term insurance statute. Some states have no specific requirements for licensing at all but require an application be submitted with information about the nature and scope of business activity along with other information.

The licensing requirements in some states include minimum financial net worth, minimum net premiums written, minimum surplus, and minimum surety bond. State laws typically require a broker to be licensed as an agent or as a corporate entity.

Many insurance companies are not familiar with the laws governing freight brokerage business so it is best to consult your insurance broker or attorney before you enter this industry. This will help you save time and money by not endangering your investments.

The main regulators that you should be aware about are:

1. Federal Motor Carrier Safety Administration (FMCSA)

This is the main regulatory body for all freight brokers. They are responsible for making sure that the freight brokers operate in accordance with their set of standards and rules.

They have the authority to take actions against unethical businesses.

2. Department of Transportation (DOT)

This is another regulatory body that regulates the operations of freight brokers. This body disposes of the policies and procedures that govern how a freight broker should operate. They also make sure that the company is following the laws and regulations set out by FMCSA.

3. Federal Communications Commission (FCC)

When you are planning to offer transportation services, it is important to know what rules you need to follow regarding radio frequencies. The FCC provides guidelines on this so therefore it is important for you as a business owner to understand their jurisdiction over your business activities inside and outside your state or country.

4. State Regulatory Authority

This body is responsible for enforcing and making sure that the freight brokers are following the standards set by DOT and FMCSA. They also help freight brokers to get licensed by federal government authorities. When you are starting a business, it is important to follow the rules in your state.

5. Federal Trade Commission (FTC)

This is another regulatory body that ensures that all freight brokers play fair in their business practices. They make sure that the freight brokers are not misleading their clients with false advertising or any other means of defrauding them. They also ensure that they are not engaging in any unfair trade practices such as price fixing or unfair competition with other competitors in the marketplace. In addition, they make sure that these companies follow all consumer laws regarding fraud and deception when dealing with their clients or their competition.

6. Equal Employment Opportunity Commission (EEOC)

They regulate fair employment practices among freight brokers across the country including discrimination based on gender, age, race, or national origin, among others. In this way they ensure equal employment opportunities for everyone. For a company to be successful, therefore, it is important to comply with the laws set by these bodies.

7. Department of Labor (DOL)

They are responsible for enforcing the rules for labor and employment that governs every freight broker. This includes the minimum wage, among other things. In addition, they make sure that the freight brokers are providing their workers with adequate health and other benefits as required by law. The goal is to ensure that all people working in this company are covered under a legally binding contract and also that they get paid all the benefits due to them as required by law.

8. Department of Energy (DOE)

They regulate transportation of dangerous materials such as gasoline, propane, and others which are used to power trucks, among other vehicles. They ensure that all rules regarding transportation of such dangerous goods are followed strictly by all freight brokers across the country for safety purposes. In this way, the government tries to safeguard the lives of the people living in areas where these dangerous goods are transported and stored temporarily or permanently depending on circumstance. The federal government makes sure that there is proper labeling of such materials so that people can take care when moving them from one place to another. Therefore, it is important for freight brokers to take care that they comply with the rules set by DOE when transporting these dangerous goods.

9. Department of Homeland Security (DHS)

They regulate all transportation of hazardous materials, dangerous goods, and other products that are transported across the country. This is to ensure that such products do not pose danger to the people living in certain parts of the country. In addition, DHS regulates companies that transport such dangerous goods across the country especially when they intend to cross state borders. Therefore, freight brokers must be aware of this regulation and ensure that they comply with it so as to avoid prosecution by DHS.

10. Department of Defense (DOD)

This department is responsible for regulating all military shipments which include freight brokers who are contracted to do so on behalf of DOD as well as those who transport such shipments on their own initiative and not contracted by DOD. They make sure that these shipments are secured at all times from any form of breach in security leading to danger to the general public. This applies to when the shipment passes through states or is temporarily stored in any state for some time before being moved on from one place to another further away from where it was originally shipped. They also make sure that there is proper labeling of such shipments and that they are properly stored in the freight brokers' facilities or any other form of storage facility.

11. Environmental Protection Agency (EPA)

They regulate all transportation of hazardous materials that are transported across the country. This is to ensure that such products delivered do not pose danger to the people living in certain parts of the country. In addition, EPA regulates companies that transport such dangerous goods across the country especially when they intend to cross state borders. Therefore, freight brokers must be aware of this regulation and ensure that they comply with it so as to avoid prosecution by EPA.

Chapter 4: Operating Your Freight Brokerage Company

Operating your freight brokerage company involves many details. Most important are the customers that you will serve and the service you provide them. You will establish your operating procedures and methods that will be used in providing high quality service to your customers.

If you can put together an excellent operation, you will be rewarded with an excellent reputation. You should be able to ask for a higher level of compensation from your customers. Customers will always give a high level of compensation if they feel highly satisfied with the service they receive.

And finally, if you have an excellent reputation and high compensation rates, it will be easier to attract new customers and expand your business. As your business expands, you will be able to hire more experienced employees.

Let's discuss the different aspects of operating your freight broker business.

Managing Your Freight Brokerage Company

Managing your freight brokerage company is not easy. In fact many of the people that get started in the business of freight brokering end up closing down their businesses within a year. The reason for this is they did not do their homework before they started and they did not have a plan.

You may have thought that you could learn the freight brokerage business on the run, but this is one business you cannot do that in. It takes a lot of time and effort to build up your freight brokerage company. You need to be able to get freight agents on board with your company in order to make money. You will also need to develop a strong working relationship between your own agents and shippers that use them.

There are five key areas that you need to focus on when you are managing your freight broker company:

1. The Shippers

You need to develop strong relationships with your shippers. You need to build trust with them and you need to treat them well. If they have a problem and you aren't able to deal with it in a timely manner, they will quickly transfer their business to another freight broker.

The shippers are the ones that provide you with a steady stream of business, so it is important that you always keep them happy.

If you are having trouble getting the shippers to agree to your service level agreement, the best thing you can do is get a copy of their current freight broker's contract and include these terms in your own. You may even be able to get them to pay a little more for the service level agreement.

For example, if their current freight broker is charging them $20 per load to get a load on time, you can charge them $25 or even $30 per load for your service level agreement. This increase in price will make you more money every month.

2. Your Freight Agent

Your freight agent is the one that finds your shipper loads and arranges for them to be picked up. You need to work with your freight agent and you need to treat them well. If they are not making as much money as they want, they will leave your company and go over to another one that can provide them with more money.

They are the one that actually does most of the work for your freight broker company and you need to remember that. If they aren't happy, they won't be working hard for you and things will go wrong. Make sure that you don't run your freight broker company like a dictator. You need to work with your agents and make sure that they are happy.

For example, if you are having a hard time getting shippers to agree to your service level agreements, you can offer to pay your freight agents more money for keeping the load on time. This extra profit will help them make more money and they will work harder for you.

3. The Freight Forwarders

The freight forwarder is the person that you will need to work with to ship your freight. You need to develop a good relationship with the freight forwarders and you need to treat them well.

If you are shipping overseas, it will be the freight forwarder that arranges for your shipment to be shipped overseas. You would want them to make a good profit on the shipment so that they will want to use your company again.

If you are shipping within the U.S., it will be the freight forwarder that arranges for your shipment to be picked up and delivered. If they are happy with your service, they may recommend you to other shippers and they may even recommend your company when their employees leave and look for new jobs in another company.

4. The Regulators

If you are going to be a freight broker, you need to be aware of all of the regulations that your company needs to follow. If you aren't following the regulations, you can be put out of business.

You need to make sure that your freight broker's license is up-to-date and that you are registered with the Federal Motor Carrier Safety Administration and the National Motor Freight Traffic Association. You will also want to make sure that you know how much insurance coverage your company needs.

5. Your Employees

When it comes right down to it, your employees may be the most important part of your business. You need them in order for your freight broker company to run smoothly and effectively. If your employees don't do their job properly, it can have a huge impact on your business and it can even put you out of business if things aren't done right.

Your employees can really make or break your company so you have to handle them with care and make sure that they are happy and feel like they are part of the company. Most of your employees will be independent contractors and you won't be able to tell them where to go or how to do their jobs. You have to trust them and let them do their jobs.

If you are new in the freight broker business, you should take some time to read about the history of what it takes to run a successful freight broker business. You should also take some time to learn about all of the rules and regulations that your company has to follow. It can be expensive if you don't know what you are doing.

Maintaining Your Freight Brokerage Company

After you have successfully established a freight broker company, you will need to maintain it. This will require that your company operate on a daily basis. To ensure that your business continues to operate successfully, you will need to make sure that you have the proper staff in place.

Employee Management:

Once you have hired your employees, you will need to make sure that they are performing their duties properly. This will allow them to continue their employment with your company. For example, if an employee is not performing their duties properly, then they should be terminated immediately. The same can be said of any employee who is stealing from the company or who is stealing from a client. Whatever the case may be, it will be necessary for you to handle these problems immediately. Otherwise, you may find yourself losing valuable clients and money if you do not take care of these issues quickly enough.

If you are having trouble finding the employees that you need, then you should consider using an online staffing company to help you. This type of company can be a great resource for finding the employees that you need to help your company grow and thrive.

For example, when you are first starting out, you may not have the resources in place to provide your employees with the benefits that they need to be successful. This can include paid time off, health insurance, and other benefits. In this case, you can hire an online staffing company to help you find freight brokers who are willing to work a certain number of hours per week in exchange for a salary or hourly wage. This can help you cover the cost of these benefits while your company is still growing.

It is also important that you look at the total compensation package that each employee receives when hiring them. This will allow you to make sure that each employee is receiving a fair wage for their services and that they are prime candidates for future growth within your company.

Company Growth:

After your freight broker business has been established, it will be necessary for your business to grow over time. If you want to ensure that this happens, then it will be necessary for you to focus on marketing and expanding your business.

For example, you should be marketing your freight services to new customers on a regular basis. This can include sending out press releases and newsletters to businesses that may be interested in your services. You can also consider advertising in a local newspaper or magazine. These are all great ways of getting your name out to the public so that they are aware of what you have to offer them.

If you want to establish a solid relationship with your clients, then you should also consider offering them a variety of freight services. These services can include anything from moving their goods from one location to another to helping them secure transportation for their goods overseas. There are many other types of additional services that may be beneficial for your clients as well. If you make these options available, it will be easier for you to meet the needs of your clients and for them to remain loyal customers in the future.

This is also a great way for you to attract new customers as well through word-of-mouth advertising. Once you have satisfied a client, they are more likely to recommend your services to others as well. This can help you to expand your business and grow your customer base over time.

Business growth is something that you should always be thinking about when starting and maintaining a freight brokerage business. If you do not have the proper marketing in place, then it will be difficult for you to grow the business as much as possible over time.

After you have established your business, you will need to maintain it and continue to grow. These are the key things that you need to have in place to ensure that your business continues to be successful over time.

Customer Service:

You will need to make sure that you are providing your clients with the best possible service. This will help to ensure that they remain loyal customers in the future and that they are willing to continue using your services.

You can provide excellent customer service by doing several different things. First of all, you should try to make sure that you are always on time when meeting with a client. If you do not show up on time for an appointment, then this could send a message to your customers about how reliable you are. In turn, this could result in clients choosing to do business with other freight brokers instead of yours.

When you are meeting with clients at their place of business, it is also important that you treat them as if they are your most important client even though their company may be small compared to others. This will help them feel like they matter and that they have received your full attention during the meeting. This can also help them feel more comfortable with the services that you provide.

In addition, you should also make sure that your clients feel like they are part of the team. This can be achieved by hosting client appreciation events on a regular basis. These events will help to build stronger relationships with your customers and make them feel more welcome to your company.

Finally, you should always make sure that the client feels valued. To do this, you should try to follow up with your clients after each meeting. This can help to ensure they have received the services they needed and that you have answered their questions in a timely manner.

Business Relationships:

It is also important that you maintain a good relationship with other freight brokers. This will help to ensure that your company is working with one of the best companies in the industry. It will also help you to ensure that you are getting the best possible deals on freight.

For example, if you are working with a new freight broker, then it may be a good idea to establish some type of cross-referral program. This can help you to grow your business while also ensuring that your clients receive the best services possible from another freight broker or trucking company. In addition, it can help to build a stronger relationship between your company and their business as well.

You can also establish relationships with other freight brokers and trucking companies by attending industry events such as conferences and trade shows. These events will give you an opportunity to meet new people who work in the industry and may provide you with new business opportunities as well.

In addition, you can also use online freight forums to contact other freight brokers and trucking companies. This can be a great way to reach out to companies that you do not necessarily know and ask them questions about their services. It will also help to build relationships between your company and other freight brokers in the industry.

Software:

While it is possible to run a freight broker business without using software, it will be necessary for you to use software in order to operate your business effectively. Freight broker software will help you to manage your freight brokerage business more efficiently and effectively. This will allow you to keep your company running smoothly while also providing you with an opportunity to grow your company in the future.

For example, some of the most important types of freight broker software that you should consider using include:

Freight Broker Software – This type of software can help you to track shipments and manage the freight brokerage side of your business. It can also help with communication between different members of your team including yourself, drivers, and clients. In addition, this type of software can help you to keep track of expenditures in order to ensure that they are all being accounted for properly.

Freight Broker CRM Software – This type of software can be used as a customer relationship management system that allows you to keep track of your clients. It will allow you to keep track of each client's needs and wants. For example, you can use it to make notes about a particular client's preferred shipping dates. Then, when you are arranging shipments with this client, you can easily schedule the shipment to arrive during the time that they need it. This type of software can also be used for tracking your most important clients so that you know who to contact when you have a new shipment that is ready for them to pick up.

Freight Broker Dispatch and Tracking Software – This type of software can be used to keep track of your drivers and their deliveries. It will allow you to make sure that each driver is making their deliveries on time and in a safe manner. You can also use it to ensure that your trucking company is being paid on time for the services they provide or have provided in the past. This may include things such as fuel costs, parking costs, or other costs related to keeping your trucks on the road.

Freight Broker Accounting Software – This type of software can be used to keep track of all accounting related aspects of the freight brokerage company. For example, you can use it to make sure that your invoices are being paid on time. You can also use it to ensure that your drivers are getting paid on time for any loads they have transported or are about to transport in the future. This will help you to keep track of all of your expenditures, revenues, and profits.

Handling Your Day-to-day Operations

Your freight brokerage company may be a sole proprietorship, partnership, corporation, or LLC. Regardless of the type of business structure that you choose, you will need to keep the day-to-day operations running smoothly. You will also need to pay your employees and vendors.

Here are some ways to handle the daily operations of your freight brokerage company:

1. Hold regular staff meetings

You should hold regular meetings with your employees and management team to discuss important company issues such as customer service, product deliveries and marketing. It is also a good idea to hold weekly staff meetings where you can talk about day-to-day operations and questions that arise during the week.

For example, let's say that you have a new freight broker who is working with a carrier to get a load delivered. This new freight broker has not had much experience with the carrier. You may want to have a weekly staff meeting where you can talk about this specific situation and the steps that the freight broker should take to help resolve any issues or concerns that arise between your company and the carrier.

2. Set up a management system

You should set up an organized management system within your freight brokerage company. You will be able to delegate responsibilities to each member of your staff so they know exactly what their job duties are and what is expected of them when it comes to their job responsibilities. As an example, you could set up one employee as the controller, another employee as the bookkeeper, and another employee as the sales manager. This will give each employee their own specific area of expertise, so they can focus on doing their jobs well and increase productivity in your company.

3. Keep your employees well-informed

You should make sure that you keep all of your employees well-informed about what is going on with the company. You may want to have regular meetings with your employees to discuss the company's finances, customer complaints, and new customers. This will help your employees understand the importance of their job and how it helps the overall operation of your freight brokerage company.

If you are a sole proprietor or a single member LLC, then you have to be the one who keeps everyone informed within your company. You can do this by speaking at staff meetings or by keeping good notes during discussions with employees. You should also keep good records of all important information that is passed along to each employee in your company.

This is important as this will help to increase productivity, overall customer service, and keep employees on track with their general work duties.

4. Set up an organized system for invoicing customers

You should set up an organized system for billing customers or clients. You may want to use a computerized invoicing system, where you can send invoices via email to your customers. You will also need to set up a good system for recording when each invoice is paid and how much was paid by each customer. This will help you keep track of your company's cash flow and make sure that you are getting regular payments from your customers.

If you do not have an organized system for invoicing customers, you will most likely have to spend a lot of time chasing payments from your customers. This can be very time consuming and can also affect the overall productivity of your freight brokerage company.

5. Set up a qualified credit policy

You should set up a good credit policy within your freight brokerage company. You need to decide early on if you want to give credit to any customers or carriers that are new to you. You will also need to decide how much credit you are willing to give each customer or carrier.

For example, if you do not know much about a new customer who calls and wants freight services, then you may want to give them only a limited amount of credit until they pay their outstanding invoices from previous shipments that they have had delivered by your company. If you do not set up some sort of criteria for giving credit within your business, then it could cause your business a great deal of financial problems in the future.

6. Maintain regular communication with your customers and carriers

You should maintain regular communication with your customers and carriers. It is important to keep up a good relationship with both of these groups of people, so they know that you are there to help them acquire freight and deliver it to their desired location.

You will also need to maintain good business relationships with your customers in order to ensure that they work closely with you when it comes to getting freight for them at a reasonable rate. This will help you get more business from customers in the future and keep your current customers happy.

You can make use of email, phone calls, or faxes to maintain good communication with your customers. You can also send letters, newsletters, or fliers to keep them informed about your company and what you do. This will help to increase customer retention and improve overall customer service.

7. Maintain good relationships with the regulators

You should maintain good relationships with the regulators. This includes the Department of Transportation, Department of Motor Vehicles, and the Federal Motor Carrier Safety Administration. These groups can help you build a good reputation within your community, as they can help you get more business by sending out information about your company to their members. If you do not have a friendly relationship with these agencies, then it could come back and hurt your overall business in the future.

For example, a good way to maintain a good relationship with these regulators is to keep up to date with the regulations that they put into place. This will help you to put in place an effective compliance program within your business. This will also help you to make sure that your business is operating according to federal and state regulations. You can also attend educational seminars and other events that are hosted by these groups, which will allow you to network with other trucking professionals in the same area as you.

8. Keep good records of your company's finances

You should keep good records of your company's finances. It is important to keep track of all expenses and revenues so you know exactly where your money is going at all times. You should use good management software for this purpose, so you can enter in all of your transactions for the day, week, or even month. This will allow you to see what areas of your business are making money and what areas are losing money so you can make adjustments accordingly.

Providing Your Customers with Great Customer Service

Great customer service is the key to success in any business, and your freight broker business is no different.

You want to make sure that you are providing great customer service by being accessible to your customers. You want to be available to them on the phone or by email at all times. This will help you with maintaining good communication and it will also help you provide them with great customer service.

Also, when they need something done, you want to make sure that it gets done as quickly as possible. It will show them that you are available and responsible for any issues that may arise and that their needs are important to you and your company.

Having a good reputation:

Having a good reputation is extremely important for anyone who wants success in their freight broker business. You want customers to know what kind of company you run and what kind of person you are through word-of-mouth advertising. This can be done by having happy customers who tell their friends about your business and services.

If you have a good reputation, your company will continue to thrive because people will know who you are and they will be willing to use your services. You need to make sure that you are always conducting business in a way that is honest, ethical, and professional in order to ensure that you have a great reputation.

Here are the top tips to help you make sure that you are providing your customers with great service and building a good reputation:

1. Be accessible to your customers:

Make sure that you are available to your customers as much as possible. They will know that you are reliable and trustworthy if you are consistently available for them. A good example of this is making sure that you have your cell phone with you at all times in case they need to contact you.

2. Always be honest and trustworthy:

You want to make sure that you are always being honest and trustworthy with your customers and clients, so they know that they can count on you for great customer service. You want to be straightforward and honest with them every step of the way. This will help establish trust between you and your customers.

3. Be considerate of your customers:

When providing customer service for your business, always be considerate of the fact that these people are using their own time to help out their company by using your freight broker services. Make sure you are being respectful of their time by always being on time, staying organized, and knowing what needs to get done when it needs to get done. These things will show them that you are responsible for any issues that may arise within your business and it will also show them that you are respectful of their time.

These are the top tips for providing your customers with great service and having a good reputation for your freight broker business.

Generating Leads and Closing Business

In order to start a freight brokerage business, you will need to generate leads and close some deals. Your leads can come from several sources.

It is recommended that you contact all the carriers in your local area. The carriers will usually be quite helpful in referring freight business to you. Depending on the size of your market, you may have several carriers to contact.

Some brokers will also take a more proactive approach by contacting potential clients directly and offering services. Most of these leads will come from businesses seeking transportation services on a regular basis, or from shippers who are considering outsourcing their transportation needs. One of the most common mistakes made by new brokers is not having any leads or not being prepared for leads when they do arrive. This can be avoided by maintaining good relationships with other companies within your market area. When it comes time for them to ship their own freight, they will look for someone who knows their company and they can trust to handle their shipments. You can also use newspaper advertisements and trade journals to generate leads. This is a very effective way to reach your target market.

How do you close deals? When lead generation is handled properly, you will soon have a steady stream of leads coming in. Most of these leads will not result in any business for you, but some will. You should always treat all leads as though they were going to be closed. If you handle them correctly, they will be closed and you can start making money!

You should always go beyond the lead by:

1. Following up with a phone call

This step is very important. Many leads will go nowhere, but a good portion of them will. If you want to make any money, you must follow up with the leads that look good.

2. Making an appointment

When you call the lead back, you should set up an appointment to meet with them and discuss their shipping needs. It is very important that you be prompt for this meeting as well. If they have to wait too long for your arrival, they may simply forget about the meeting and never contact you again. This is a common occurrence with new brokers trying to start a freight brokerage business without experience or knowledge of how to handle these leads properly.

3. Following up after the meeting

After your meeting has concluded, it is important that you follow up with the potential client in a timely manner. You should send out all quotes or proposals within one business day of the meeting and make sure to include all of the information they requested on the lead sheet for their shipment.

4. Following up after seven days

If you have not heard from the potential client, it is important to follow up with them again in a timely manner. If they still haven't responded, it is time to take action by calling them and following up once again. This continued follow-up is important because they may not have received your proposal or quote and may just be busy at the time you sent it out. If they still do not respond after repeated and timely follow ups, it may be time to move on to another lead. This is also a common occurrence with new brokers trying to start a freight brokerage business without experience or knowledge of how to handle these leads properly.

5. Following up after fourteen days

Some brokers will send a third or fourth quote if necessary, but this should be done as a last resort. It can be very annoying for people who have already been followed up with several times by the same company. If this becomes necessary you should call the customer and explain the situation and assure them that they are your first priority. You should also be prepared with a new lead at this time.

Taking Care of Your Existing Clients

It is a common mistake to neglect your existing clients in the excitement of getting new business. Always remember that if you are attracting new business, you are probably also retaining current business. Do not forget about them and certainly do not neglect them.

Remember that it is important to make sure that your clients are happy with the service they get from you and that they can get in touch with you easily if they need to. Make sure that you keep your customers informed as to what is happening with their shipments.

If you have had a problem with a shipment or there was an error in the way it was handled, tell them exactly what happened and how it has been put right. If something has gone wrong, don't say "sorry" —fix it! If a shipment has been delayed for some reason, find out why and fix it so that it doesn't happen again. The same goes for any other mistakes or problems: get them fixed before they become big problems!

Here are the top tips for keeping your clients happy:

1. Send them a regular newsletter or email to keep them up to date on your business.

This will give them a great feeling of how enthusiastic you are about your business and it will boost their confidence that they are dealing with someone who knows what they are doing.

2. Invite them to come and see your office and warehouse.

Make sure that you have a good reason for this; don't just invite them for a coffee because it will not impress them! It needs to be something that will do some good for both you and your client. Perhaps they would like to look at some new equipment or discuss a new service that you are offering. It is a good idea to make sure that the visit coincides with something special going on—perhaps an exhibition or similar—so they can see some of the other potential clients in the area as well. Keep it short and sweet, but try to get as much business out of it for yourself as possible.

3. Make sure that they know what you are doing for them.

If you have just delivered a shipment to them, send them a quick email to let them know that it has arrived safely. They will appreciate this because they will not have to worry about what is happening with their shipment. If something goes wrong with a shipment, make sure that you tell them exactly what happened and how it has been put right. This way they will be more likely to trust you with future shipments and you will build up your reputation as someone who can deliver the goods.

4. Show an interest in your clients' business.

If you are dealing with a small company, find out what other services they need from your company and offer to provide them! This is the way that great relationships are built—by putting yourself out there and being willing to help your clients in any way that you can. If their business grows, it may well become a great source of new business for you too!

5. Give them a discount if they are good clients.

If you have had a client for a long time and they have always paid you on time, it is worth giving them a discount now and again. This way they will be keen to get more work from you and their loyalty will be increased because of this. Make sure that you are not giving out too many discounts, though—it is important to make sure that your business is profitable!

6. Offer something extra for free when business has been good.

As well as discounts, you can offer something extra as a sign of thanks for their business; perhaps some promotional items with your logo on or an extra service that they might not really need—but will be glad to have! It is also worth making sure that you send thank-you cards with shipments to say thank you for the business; this will give people a great feeling of what kind of person you are and how much thought goes into everything that your company does.

7. Thank people when they have recommended you to others.

If a client has recommended you to another company and business has come in as a result, make sure that you thank them and let them know how much business the recommendation has brought in. This will reward them for their loyalty to you and encourage them to recommend more clients for you in the future.

8. Send birthday or anniversary cards with gifts—but don't send too many!

You can send birthday cards and anniversary cards as long as they are relevant to your clients' business. These will give your clients a great feeling of how much effort goes into their business by your company—but don't go overboard, otherwise it will seem tacky! It is also worth finding out what their hobbies or interests are so that you can tailor the card accordingly; this way they will be even more impressed by your attention to detail and the effort that goes into each shipment from start to finish!

Establishing Yourself as a Thought Leader in Your Industry

You must be able to establish yourself as a leader in your industry. In fact, you are the thought leader in your industry. You know your industry like no one else. You are the freight broker expert and should act like it. This requires you to know how to position yourself as the expert in your industry.

You must have an opinion on every aspect of your industry. You must change with the changing business climate, and take a leadership role within it. Your opinions must be relevant, so that when other people read them they will think "that makes sense." Of course, you also need to have some credibility behind those opinions for them to actually matter. This is where your experience comes into play.

Your opinions can come from any source: news articles or industry studies, for example; but they should always be written as if they were your own thoughts and never plagiarized from anyone else's words or thoughts (which we all know is wrong). As such, if you write a blog post about any subject, it should be your own words and thoughts.

As you start to develop your own thoughts and opinions, they will go through a trial by fire. People will dismiss your ideas, or even insult them; but they will not be able to deny their validity. As such, you will be seen as an expert in your industry. Your credibility as the expert will also grow with every article you write for your blog and every speech you give at events or conferences in your industry.

Before long people in your industry will start to call you up for advice on how to do things in their business. You can then use that opportunity to offer them advice on how they can apply that same advice directly to their business if they work with you as a customer of yours or even as one of your subcontractors (in which case they would become affiliates of yours). This is where the word-of-mouth marketing starts to take place that can drive people into doing business with you.

You should also start to use your expert status as a means to get yourself on television, in magazines, or on the radio. You can then use those media appearances as a way to promote your website and blog articles.

As you continue to build your reputation as an expert in the industry, people will be willing to pay handsomely for your advice and recommendations. You can then use that opportunity to charge a fee for consultations and speeches that you give at industry events or conferences. Those fees will help offset the cost of running your business and allow you to make money while you sleep (or do something else). This is how most successful businesses are run: they are built upon a foundation of providing products or services where the money is made outside of the products or services themselves.

You can also use those consulting fees as another way to find more business opportunities by giving them away free of charge to customers who are referred by customers who have already paid for consulting services from you. This not only builds your relationship with existing customers, but it also builds relationships with new customers.

The following is the outline for how to establish yourself as a thought leader in your industry, and how that will lead to more consulting opportunities for you:

Step 1: Build Your Credibility

Start blogging about your industry. Write about what you know, and write about it as an expert. You can start by reading the news about your industry and writing your opinion on those news articles.

It is also a good idea to review and comment on books, blogs, and videos that talk about your industry. You can also offer advice on industry-related questions posed by other people on forums or social media sites like Twitter.

Step 2: Build Your Reputation

Continue blogging about your industry. Continue to write about what you know, and continue to write as an expert in the industry. When you make a prediction about something in the future, be sure to follow up with an article that explains how you were right or wrong about that prediction (if you were wrong). This will allow others to learn from your predictions, and it will keep any predictions you make in the future more credible when they come true (which will help build your reputation as an expert).

Don't be afraid to take a position on topics that are controversial in your industry. Controversy is an attention-getter, and that's what you need to be if you want people to listen to what you have to say.

Step 3: Build Your Brand

When it comes time for you to speak at a conference or event in your industry, charge for your speaking fee. Make sure that the event will give you the opportunity to do a lot of marketing of yourself and your blog in the days leading up to your speech as well as during your speech itself.

After each of these events, mention them on your blog and mention the number of people who attended the event as well as their names and companies (if possible). This will help you build credibility with those people because they will be able to see that they are not just hearing from some anonymous person, but instead they are hearing from someone who is respected by their peers in their industry. This can be a great way for them to get some long-term business from those peers.

Step 4: Build Your Business

As your credibility and reputation grows, you will begin to receive requests for consulting services from people in your industry who want you to help them solve problems that they are having with their business. You can charge a fee for those consulting services and use those fees to help offset the cost of running your business.

For example, if you are asked to help someone find a new freight broker, you can take a fee for giving them the name of several freight brokers that you know well. If you are asked to help someone find a new sales agent, you can take a fee for giving them the name of several sales agents that you know well. You can also build your business by offering consulting services to people who need help with marketing or even with hiring employees.

You can also charge an hourly consulting fee for speaking engagements where people will want to pick your brain about things in your industry.

As your reputation and credibility grows, you will also begin to receive requests for speeches at industry events and conferences. You can charge an honorarium or speaking fee for each speech that you give at an event or conference in your industry.

Chapter 5: Scaling Your Freight Brokerage Company

Scaling your freight brokerage company, as you have seen in the previous chapters, is a matter of taking calculated steps to move toward the goals that you have set. Scaling is a process and it is not something that can be taken lightly.

There are a lot of variables that come in play with scaling your freight brokerage company. Some of them are out of your control while others are very much under your control. It is important to realize that there will be some challenges along the way and you need to be ready to face them head on; they will not go away just because you ignore them.

With all this said, this chapter will give you some direction on how to scale your freight brokerage company successfully and how to avoid some of the common problems that can occur when scaling a freight brokerage company.

That being said, before we get started looking at how to scale your freight brokerage company, let's look at why it is important for us to even consider scaling our business.

Take Your Freight Broker Business to the Next Level

As a freight broker, you are in a position of power. Freight brokers have both the power to buy freight and the power to sell freight. This in itself gives you some pretty good leverage in the industry.

The problem is that most freight brokers only use this leverage when they are buying or selling freight. They tend to be focused on getting the best possible deal on a single transaction but they do not take advantage of their position to grow their business further.

Freight brokers need to realize that with their unique position, they can scale their business very quickly and very easily if they are willing to take the time and put in the effort needed for it. It is very easy for them to grow their business in terms of revenue but also in terms of profitability as well if they are willing to take what we are going to talk about below and apply it into their daily operations.

There are many different ways for a freight broker to increase revenue, profits, and growth for his or her freight brokerage company.

The key to this is to have a good plan and understanding of what you are doing and why you are doing it. If you have this, then scaling your freight brokerage company should not be a problem at all.

It is important for you to understand that if your goal is to just become the biggest freight broker in town, then chances are that you will fail at this endeavor because there will always be someone bigger than you. But if your goal is to build a profitable business with sustainable growth, then you will not only succeed at achieving your goals but also in growing your business beyond what anyone would ever expect.

So, without further ado, let's get started and look at how we can scale our freight brokerage company successfully and efficiently.

How to Grow Your Freight Brokerage Company

You've done the hard part. You've started a freight brokerage company and you're making money. You think you can do it on your own, but as your business grows, you will need to hire more employees and utilize outside services. This is a natural progression as well as an important one to keep your costs down and maximize profits.

As you grow, there are several ways in which you can calculate the best way to scale your business. These include:

1. Hiring employees to take over parts of your business.

Your employees are an extremely important part of your business. They can help you grow, streamline processes, and save you time and money. Many businesses start out with a single employee and add to their staff as needed. Once you reach a certain point, you will need to hire employees to take over specific tasks.

For example, if you do not have a marketing or sales department, you will hire someone to handle sales. If you are drowning in paperwork and your back office is a mess, the easiest way to fix it is by hiring someone who specializes in that area.

Some business owners may feel uncomfortable hiring employees. They may feel that it is beneath them to hire people to take over a task they can do themselves. However, this is one of the best ways to run your freight brokerage company. By hiring employees, you will free up your time to focus on the areas that need your attention more.

Doing so will allow you to grow your business to the next level.

2. Use outsourcing services to handle certain tasks.

Another way to scale your business is to use outsourcing services. This can include tax services, technology support, accounting services, and many more. Think of it as renting space in a shared office or business center. When you outsource a task, you can hire someone from outside your company on an as-needed basis instead of hiring an employee for that specific task.

The best way to use outsourcing services is to hire a virtual assistant. A virtual assistant can take over many of the menial tasks that you don't want to do yourself. Also, if you have a business with multiple employees, you can hire a virtual assistant to take over tasks that only one person can do. This helps keep your back office running smoothly and frees up your employees to focus on their core responsibilities.

3. Consider hiring a consultant for advice or help with growing your business.

If you want outside assistance but are uncomfortable with the idea of hiring an employee, consider hiring a business consultant. Business consultants work on a one-time basis and can help you figure out where you need to grow or where your business needs more help.

Another benefit of hiring a consultant is that they are often brought in as an outside expert to get the job done right. This means that they will have no emotional ties to the company, which means they will be able to give you unbiased advice on how to grow your freight brokerage company without worrying about what is best for them.

If you want outside advice but would prefer not to bring in additional staff members, a consulting service may be a good option for your freight brokerage company.

4. Launch an aggressive marketing campaign and grow your brand recognition.

When it comes to growth, many businesses start out small because they don't know how else to expand their brand recognition. The best way to expand your freight brokerage brand is by launching an aggressive marketing campaign. This can include social media ads, Google Ads, or any other strategy that will put your business on the map.

Another benefit of launching an aggressive marketing campaign is that you will start to get more leads. As your business grows, you will need a way to manage all of the incoming leads. The best way to do this is by using a CRM program for your freight brokerage company like CargoHub.[17]

5. Use social media and other marketing strategies to grow your freight brokerage company.

Speaking of using social media and other strategies, it is important to be as active as possible on several different platforms to increase brand awareness and drive leads for your freight brokerage business. This can include:

---

[17] CargoHub http://www.cargohub.ro/

Instagram – If you have high-quality photos and videos of your own employees or products in action, post them on Instagram and encourage users to follow you. The platform is very visual so you can make an impact with high-quality photos or short video clips as well as longer posts.

Facebook – This is one of the most popular social media platforms and a good place to get your freight brokerage company name out there. However, you must be careful how you use it because Facebook can be highly restrictive when it comes to advertising. If you don't have plenty of followers already, you may not be able to launch an aggressive marketing campaign on Facebook.

LinkedIn – This is one of the best sites for B2B companies to use because it is more professional and less social than other platforms. However, you can still post updates, connect with people, and even launch a Facebook ad campaign through LinkedIn.

Twitter – Twitter is the best place to use hashtags to find customers. If you use the right hashtags, you can reach your target audience and make a big impact on their lives without being too aggressive. However, Twitter is a very competitive platform so you may need to get your freight brokerage company name out there before you can take advantage of it.

6. Launch a referral program for your freight brokerage business.

Once you've grown your brand recognition and are getting more leads for your freight brokerage company, consider launching a referral program to reward those who refer new clients or get the word out about your business. This can include anything from offering cash rewards for referrals or even offering discounts on future services in exchange for bringing in new business.

This can be one of the most effective ways to market your freight brokerage company if you have a solid base of customers who are willing to refer new business your way. However, make sure you don't give away discounts or rewards for random referrals because this will make it harder for people to trust your company.

7. Start a membership program for your freight brokerage company.

If you want to take scaling your freight brokerage company to the next level, consider starting a membership program for both customers and employees. This is an ideal strategy for businesses that service customers but also require services from their client base in order to operate. Think of it as a subscription service like Netflix or Amazon Prime. Your freight brokerage company can offer its services at a discount in exchange for recurring membership fees.

The best way to do this is by offering different levels of membership depending on what services are included and the number of services provided at each level. Each level could have its own benefits as well. For example, at one level, you could offer discounted rates for freight brokerage services and member-only deals on other services. At a higher level, you could offer access to specialized training or even exclusive discounts for future freight brokerage services.

8. Develop a proprietary software program for your freight brokerage company.

If you are serious about growing your freight brokerage company and want to have more control over the entire process, consider developing a proprietary software program that is used by your team members as well as customers. This is great for any business that relies heavily on technology or utilizes technology in their core workflow processes because it allows you to take more control over the entire process and provide a better service than anyone else can offer.

A good way to do this is by creating an app or software program that your customers can download onto their phone or device so they can track their shipments in real time, get notifications when something changes with their shipment schedule, etc. You can then develop an extensive support system for your software program and hire support staff to help your customers get the most out of it.

9. Create a brand-new product or service to offer your freight brokerage company customers.

If you are ready to take your business to the next level, consider creating a brand-new product or service that you can offer to your current customers as well as newly acquired clients. This can help you develop a new revenue stream and ensure that you are always growing and offering the best possible solution for your freight brokerage company. For example, if one of your current services is providing warehouse storage for long-term goods, create an app that helps customers get their goods stored at a discount in exchange for a monthly membership fee.

This will take time, money, and effort but will be well worth it when it comes time to sell the business because it will have more value than other businesses in its industry.

Securing Growth Capital for a Freight Brokerage Business

It is essential to get a line of credit or a loan to start your business. Freight brokers are service providers and they do not have the ability to hold inventory for their clients. This makes it difficult to secure growth capital for your freight brokerage company. Growth capital is essential to start your freight brokerage business because it would give you flexibility and the ability to grow your business.

The best way to secure a loan or line of credit is by applying through the banks that you are already dealing with as a freight broker. Banks are familiar with freight broker businesses and would be more likely than others to provide you with the capital that you need for your business. If you do not have established banking relationships, other options that you can consider include venture capitalists, investors, or private financing companies that cater to small businesses.

Other ways of securing growth capital include obtaining funding from family and friends, contributing personal savings into the business, applying for grants, and obtaining government subsidies if there are any available to your business.

How to Get the Capital for Your Freight Brokerage Business:

Once you have decided on the type of loan or line of credit that you want to obtain to start your freight brokerage company, the next step is to secure capital. This process can be challenging because freight broker companies are not well known and banks would typically not offer the loan or line of credit without collateral.

One way to convince the bank that you are worthy of obtaining a line of credit or a loan is by providing them with your financial statements, including your personal financial statement, and showing the bank that you have sufficient funds to start your freight brokerage company.

If you have been in business before then you can also provide them with your previous financial statements to show your success as a business owner. The other way is to find an investor who will be willing to take the risk on your freight brokerage business in exchange for shares in your company. Another option is finding a private financing company who would be willing to provide you with the business capital without having any stake in your freight brokerage company.

Alternatively, you can also apply for a grant or a government subsidy if any would be available to small business owners like you. This would allow you to secure growth capital with little to no risk.

Once you have secured growth capital for your freight brokerage business, the next step is to manage it wisely and use it wisely. This is where many businesses fail because they focus more on getting the money rather than using it wisely. If you do not know how to use your growth capital properly then it would be best if you get assistance from someone who knows how to manage the funds properly. This way, you will be able to secure growth capital without losing money in the process.

Here are some of the alternative ways that you can secure capital for your freight brokerage business:

1. Family and Friends

You can ask for a loan or ask someone to invest in your freight brokerage business from your family and friends. It is easier to get money from people you know because you have a preexisting relationship with them and they can trust you enough to make the investment. However, there are a number of risks if you are going with this option. If the person or people who agreed to fund your freight brokerage business fail to see a return on their investment then they might not be willing to extend more loans or provide additional capital. This could lead to problems in the future, especially if you are not able to manage your growth capital properly.

2. Private Financing Companies

One way of securing growth capital for your freight brokerage business is by finding a private financing company that would be willing to provide funds without having any stake in the company. This is similar to borrowing money from banks because these private financing companies will also require collateral for the loan that they give out. The big difference is that this private financing company would be more lenient in the terms and conditions of the loan. They are not concerned with your personal financial situation like banks are so they would be willing to accept business collateral as a form of security for your loan.

3. Venture Capitalists

Venture capitalists are investors who seek out companies with a high growth potential and provide them with capital in exchange for shares in the company. You can approach venture capitalists to fund your freight brokerage business but this option has a number of risks as well. If you cannot manage the growth capital properly, then it might affect your venture capitalist's investment in your freight brokerage company and they might decide to take their share of the business or force you to sell it off which could lead to bankruptcy if you do not have enough income coming from the business to pay them off. This is not something you should pursue if you do not know how to handle growth capital properly. It is best that you find an experienced investor to partner with your freight brokerage company in order to ensure that you do not lose money in the process.

4. Government Funding

If you have a great business idea but are not able to secure capital for it, then you can try looking for grant programs for small businesses. There are grant programs available by the government that would provide funding for businesses that are looking to expand their operations or start a new business. You can look online and find out if there are any available grant programs or funding sources for small businesses like yours. The good thing about these grant programs is that they do not require collateral and they do not expect a return on their investment so you would be able to secure growth capital without having any risk involved. This is one of the best ways of securing growth capital because there is little risk involved and you get funds without having to give up control over your freight brokerage company.

Increasing Your Freight Brokerage Company's Revenue

Freight brokers have several ways to increase revenue from their businesses. Freight brokers are able to charge freight forwarders with a percentage of the total revenue generated or by charging a flat fee for each transaction. Freight forwarders usually prefer flat fees versus percentage fees, because they only have to pay for services they're actually using.

Freight brokers may also charge freight shippers by charging a flat fee or by charging a per pound rate, per carton rate, per container rate, or even a combination of these methods.

Freight brokers can also increase their revenue by offering additional services to both freight forwarders and shippers. Additional services include providing freight insurance, ocean transportation, air cargo transportation, and much more.

Here are the most common ways freight brokers increase their revenue:

1. Insurance

Freight brokers are able to sell insurance to both freight forwarders and shippers. Freight insurance is sold in the form of a blanket policy that covers any type of loss, damage, or delay in delivery. Providing an add-on service such as insurance is a great way to increase your freight brokerage business' revenue.

For example, a shipper might opt to purchase insurance from a freight broker in the event that their shipment gets damaged or lost in transit. Freight brokers would charge a flat fee for each policy sold in addition to the premium paid by the end user.

2. Transportation

Freight brokers are able to offer transportation services such as ocean, air, and ground transportation. To offer this service, freight brokers would need to have relationships with multiple shipping lines to benefit both themselves and their clients. Freight brokers are also able to provide additional services such as load consolidation for shippers whose shipments are too small to ship on their own.

For example, a shipper may want to send a shipment via ocean transportation but may be unable to do so because of the size of the shipment. The freight broker is able to consolidate multiple shipments into one container which can then be shipped via ocean transportation at a lower cost per pound than if each shipment was shipped individually on its own container. This allows the shipper to add extra weight to their shipment at a lower cost while still receiving fast ground transportation.

3. Third Party Logistics Service

Freight brokers are able to offer third party logistics (3PL) services for shippers and forwarders. This service allows freight brokers to manage the entire supply chain process with no interaction between the freight broker and the end user.

Freight brokers are able to charge a flat fee for offering this service or they may charge a percentage of the total revenue generated by offering this service.

For example, a shipper may want to outsource their shipping and warehousing processes so that they don't have to deal with any of the inventory or logistics themselves. This allows them to focus on their core business functions such as marketing, sales, finance, operations, etc. The shipper is then able to ship in bulk via carrier which then gets picked up by a 3PL service provided by the freight broker. The 3PL service then warehouses all products and ships each product individually to the shipper's end users.

4. Franchising

Freight brokers are able to franchise their businesses to other individuals. This allows freight brokers to expand their business without having to hire new staff or rent additional office space. Freight brokers are able to charge a flat fee for each franchise sold or they may charge a percentage of the total revenue generated by the franchisee.

For example, an established freight broker may want to expand their business but they don't want to hire new staff or rent additional office space. The freight broker is then able to sell a franchise agreement for their business so that someone else can run the business for them, while still receiving a portion of the revenue generated by the franchise. Similarly, an existing freight broker may want to open multiple locations but doesn't want to devote all of their time and effort into expanding their business. The freight broker is then able to sell multiple franchises so that other people can run separate locations for them and still receive revenue from those locations in addition to the original location.

Marketing Strategies that Grow Your Business

At a certain point, you'll realize that the marketing strategies you are currently using are no longer effective. You will need to develop new marketing programs to take your business to the next level.

This section will guide you on how to develop a marketing plan for your freight brokerage company. Scaling your business is possible once you have a solid marketing strategy in place.

Here are the ways that you can develop a solid marketing strategy for a successful freight broker business:

1. Learn from your competition:

Take the time to analyze how your competitors are marketing their freight brokerage services. Are they using online lead generation programs? Are they using Yellow Page ads? What are they doing and how are they doing it?

For example, a good way to see how your competitors are marketing is to view their websites. Are they using search engine optimization (SEO) techniques? How do they use social media? Are they using classified ads?

You can use various tools to analyze your competition, one of which is a Google Alert. You can also use a tool to compare keywords for SEO, such as Google Adwords Keyword Tool.

The point is to pay attention to what your competitors are doing and see if you can learn something from them. You can learn how they are generating leads for their freight broker business and then create similar programs for your company.

2. Develop a marketing plan:

Once you know how your competitors are marketing their freight brokerage business, you can develop a marketing plan for your own company.

A marketing plan is an essential tool that will help you identify your target market, different ways to generate leads, and how to measure the success of your programs.

Your marketing plan should list all of the different ways that you can market your freight brokerage business. The more avenues you have in place, the more successful you'll be at growing and scaling your business.

3. Create a budget:

The next step is to create a budget for all programs that were identified in the previous step. How much money will each program cost? Will this increase sales? How much will it cost if there's no increase in sales? You need to have answers to these questions before moving forward with each marketing program. Whenever possible, it's always good to start small and scale into larger programs as needed. It's better to spend a little money now and see how it works, before spending more money later.

4. Test before launching new programs:

Before going live with any new marketing programs, you'll want to test them first. You may think that the program is good, but you must always test it first before rolling out the program across your entire company. If the program doesn't receive favorable results, then you can tweak it to make it better.

5. Measure each marketing program:

One of the most important steps to scaling your freight broker business is to measure each marketing program that are being used. This way, you can see how effective each strategy is at generating leads for your freight brokerage company. You can also track how much (or how little) money is being spent on each marketing strategy and decide if this strategy should be scaled up or down in the future. This will help with determining what strategies are working and which ones aren't working for your business.

Attracting New Clients to Your Freight Brokerage Firm

New clients are the lifeblood of any freight broker business. When you are starting up your freight broker company, you will have the opportunity to attract clients from a number of different sources. The following are some of the best ways to attract new clients to your freight broker company.

It is very important that you build a strong and thick pipeline of potential clients. This is important as it mitigates the risk of experiencing a fall in sales.

The following is a list of the best ways to attract new clients to your freight broker business.

1. Have a bundle promotion

It is important that you have a bundle promotion as this is one of the best ways to attract clients to your freight broker business. A bundle promotion is where you offer a number of services at an affordable rate. This offers your clients the opportunity to save on costs as they can subscribe to your freight broker service at a discounted price.

This works because it allows you to get the attention of potential clients. If you are able to offer more services at a discounted price, this makes your freight broker firm more attractive to clients.

For example, if you are planning to invite clients to join your freight broker business, you should consider offering them a bundle promotion. Offering a bundle promotion is a great way to attract potential clients.

2. Send direct mail

Direct mail is one of the best ways to attract new clients to your freight broker company. When you send direct mail to prospective clients, you will have the opportunity to create a brand for your freight broker business.

In order for this strategy to work, it is important that you include your brand in the direct mail. This allows clients to get an insight into your business and it gives you an opportunity to create trust in your brand.

It is also essential that you design direct mail pieces that are eye-catching and appealing. This allows you to get the attention of potential clients who are looking for a freight broker service provider.

Unprofessional looking direct mail pieces will not be effective as they will not help shape the image of your freight broker business. Your potential clients will look at quality and professionalism when it comes to choosing a freight broker service provider. Make sure that you use professional looking materials when designing your direct mailing campaigns as this could be very important when it comes to getting new clients to your freight broker business.

3. Host a seminar

Another great way to attract new clients to your freight broker business is by hosting a seminar. If you are planning to host a seminar, it is important that you provide a good and interesting platform for your clients.

It is very important that you choose the right venue for your seminar as this could have an impact on the number of people who attend the event. Make sure that the venue has enough seating capacity and that it is comfortable. This will ensure that you get enough people to attend your seminar.

When it comes to hosting your seminar, make sure that you choose a topic that is relevant to your audience. The topic should be highly relevant and interesting in nature. This will allow you to keep the audience engaged throughout the duration of the event. The topics should also help promote your business as well as educate prospective clients about freight broker services in general.

Chapter 6: Regulations and Certification

The creation of a freight brokerage company gives you the chance to start your own company that will represent and help other businesses. This is why it is important that you get all the necessary certification as well as learn about the proper regulations to follow. You can find more information on these topics in this guide.

Before you start creating a business, it is important for you to get the proper knowledge of the regulations in your state. This is because these rules and regulations will be applied to your business and it is important for you to know them so you can keep your business registered.

For example, in New York City, you need to have a surety bond of $50,000, which means that if you fail to comply with the state's regulations, this bond will be used in order to compensate for any losses within the state. In addition, there are some other documents that you need to have: a freight broker license and a tax-exempt certificate.

In California, there are some specific rules that you will be following when it comes to your company's name. For example, if your company has two words in its name, then the second word can't be used as a verb. In addition, you need to put a comma between the words in your company's name.

In addition to that, if you want to call yourself a carrier representative, you will need to get a license. This is one of the most popular titles for freight brokers and it's used when you act as an intermediary between carriers and consignors.

The Legal Framework of Freight Brokerage

Freight brokerage is a regulated business. Many freight brokers are unaware of their legal responsibilities and obligations. There are two major sets of regulations that freight brokers need to be aware of: The Federal Motor Carrier Safety Regulations[18] (FMCSRs) and the Interstate Commerce Commission[19] (ICC) regulations. The FMCSRs apply to any person or business that hires out trucks and drivers or sells goods. The ICC regulations apply only if a freight broker is involved in interstate commerce.

---

18 FMCSRs https://www.fmcsa.dot.gov/regulations

19 Will Kenton (updated November 21st 2019) https://www.investopedia.com/terms/i/interstate-commerce-commission.asp

The Federal Motor Carrier Safety Regulations:

The FMCSRs are a set of regulations promulgated by the U.S. Department of Transportation (DOT) that apply to all trucking companies, their drivers, and any person or business that hires out trucks and drivers or sells goods. These regulations apply whether the transportation is interstate or intrastate in nature. The original FMCSRs were enacted in 1935 to improve motor carrier safety. They are jointly governed by the Federal Motor Carrier Safety Administration (FMCSA) and the Federal Highway Administration (FHWA).

The Interstate Commerce Commission Regulations:

The ICC is a federal agency created in 1887 whose purpose was to regulate railroads, trucking companies, and other common carriers involved in interstate commerce. This agency did not control railroads after 1995 when it was consolidated into the Surface Transportation Board. However, even though this part of its regulatory authority has been eliminated, the ICC still regulates interstate freight shipments by air, water, and pipeline. In addition to these common carriers specifically mentioned in the ICC code, any person or business that is involved in interstate commerce is also covered by the ICC regulations.

Certification Requirements:

Under the FMCSRs and ICC regulations, all persons who hold themselves out as a freight broker must be certified. The ICC regulations (49 CFR 390) require that anyone who makes an interstate offer or acceptance of freight be certified. The FMCSRs (Part 365) require that anyone who hires out trucks and drivers or sells goods be certified. This certification, which is given by state motor vehicle officials, is required before a freight broker can operate legally in the United States. A freight broker's license does not permit him to hire out trucks and drivers under the FMCSRs; it merely certifies that he has been trained and tested on aspects of transportation law, safety, and ethics pertaining to all modes of transportation (air, surface, rail). The U.S. Department of Transportation does not require that a freight broker have a physical office in the area in which he conducts business.

Advantages of Certification:

Being certified as a freight broker is not only required by law, but it also gives you an edge over your competition. Freight brokers who are certified are more likely to be considered reliable and trustworthy by their customers. This can be especially important if your customer is a large corporation that has shipping needs many times each month. A freight broker who is not certified may appear to be a fly-by-night operator that may not be around for very long, or worse yet, may not even exist!

What happens if you are not certified?

If you are caught operating as a freight broker without certification, the FMCSA can fine you up to $10,000[20] and the ICC can fine you up to $1,000. In addition, if you are not certified and are caught transporting goods or hazardous materials, both the FMCSA and the ICC can fine you up to $10,000!

Do I need a license for my business?

If your business is selling goods for others or giving others transportation services, then yes—according to the U.S. Department of Transportation. If you are not in either of these categories then you probably do not need a license. The easiest way to tell is by looking at your business activities: if they involve moving goods from one place to another (even if it is just within your own company) then you probably need a license.

---

[20] FMSCA penalty https://www.fmcsa.dot.gov/sites/fmcsa.dot.gov/files/docs/mission/information-systems/prism/404866/ufafinestable2018-final-used-ufa-manual.pdf

Licensing vs. Certification

Some business owners are confused about the difference between licensing and certification.

To help understand the difference, we will first discuss the definitions of licensing and certification:

Licensing

Licensing refers to the authorization or permission given by a government or a specific agency, in this case, the Federal Motor Carrier Safety Administration (FMCSA), to an individual, group of individuals, or business entity to undertake specified activities. Examples of activities include operating a motor carrier business and hauling goods from one place to another. The activities are authorized based on specified requirements such as training, knowledge, proficiency, physical fitness, and background checks. A licensing authority may revoke or suspend an individual's license if he/she violates any of the provisions in his/her license. A business entity's license is revoked if it does not meet its requirements such as maintaining records such as driver records for more than 60 days. Please visit Federal Motor

Carrier Safety Administration's website for more information on regulations pertaining to motor carriers.

Certification

Certification refers to an official recognition or designation by a regulatory body or an organization that a person or entity meets certain specified requirements. FMCSA, for example, issues Certified Carrier and Qualified Manager certifications to motor carriers. In the case of motor carriers, the Agency's regulations require them to have a certified manager and vehicle inspectors on staff before they are allowed to operate. Please visit Federal Motor Carrier Safety Administration's website for more information on regulations pertaining to motor carriers.

It is important to understand that license and certification are two different things. A number of business owners confuse licensing with certifications. In fact, there are even businesses operating in the industry that identify themselves as "licensed freight brokers" but they have not undergone the necessary licensure requirements.

The following is a list of common mistakes freight brokers make when it comes to licensing:

1. They use the term "license" to refer to what is actually a certification.

This is a common mistake and a very serious one. The term "license" should only be used to refer to a document issued by FMCSA that authorizes a business to operate as a motor carrier.

2. They use the term "certification" to refer to what is actually a license.

Just like the previous example, this is also a serious mistake because it confuses the business owner and his/her clients.

3. Not knowing the difference between licensing and certification, they end up applying for the wrong type of document with FMCSA.

This also happens quite often but fortunately, there are freight broker associations such as American Freight Association (AFA) that can help you get your certificate or license for free or at a small cost. Please visit American Freight Association's website for more information on how to get your license or certificate without breaking your bank account.

4. They apply for the wrong type of license or certificate.

It is common for a freight broker to apply for a carrier license when they actually need a broker license instead. It is also common to apply for a broker's license when they need a certified manager's certificate. Please keep in mind that in addition to having the correct type of license, you also have to meet the minimum requirements set by FMCSA, so make sure you know what you are getting into before you start applying for any document.

5. They do not renew their license or certificate on time.

A lot of business owners forget that they must renew their documents on time and end up paying fines because they failed to do so. In addition, not renewing your document on time can cause major problems such as you being unable to transport goods after your expiration date since FMCSA will consider your application "denied." For example, brokers who do not renew their licenses on time will have to go to court if they get pulled over by FMCSA for transporting goods.

6. They do not know which type of license or certificate they need to be eligible for certain discounts.

Freight brokers who do not have the correct type of license will not be able to access discounts such as fuel surcharge and hazardous materials discount. They will also have to pay fines if they are caught operating without a license.

7. They consider their broker's license as a substitute for other types of licenses such as a hazardous materials endorsement or a hazmat training certificate.

Each type of business has different regulations and requirements, so it is important that you know which type you need before applying for it. For example, hazardous materials endorsement is only applicable for brokers who intend on hauling hazardous materials and the only way to get this endorsement is through an approved training program from FMCSA, so if you do not intend on hauling hazmat, there is no need for you to apply for this endorsement since it will only complicate your application process and waste your time and money.

8. They believe they do not need a license because they are only transporting household goods and/or exempt commodities.

A lot of business owners think they do not need a license because they are only operating in the household goods industry and/or transporting exempt commodities such as grain, produce, and lumber. However, federal regulations require all motor carriers to be properly licensed regardless of the type of commodity they intend on hauling as long as it is for-hire. If you are caught without a license while operating freight, you will be fined and your operating authority will be suspended or revoked by FMCSA.

Freight Broker Code of Ethics

Freight brokers must always act with honesty and integrity to ensure that their actions are not misleading or deceptive. Should a freight broker ever be found guilty of any criminal offense, it must be disclosed to the industry immediately.

In order for you to become a certified freight broker, you will have to meet all the government regulations put into place for your safety and the safety of the general public. This includes having an understanding of freight forwarding laws, regulations, rules, and compliance.

For example, one regulation requires you to have a Federal Identification Number. This number is an individual taxpayer identification number that is issued by the IRS (Internal Revenue Service). The Federal ID number can be used instead of a social security number when filing your corporate income tax returns. The Federal ID number is used by the IRS to track your business activities.

In addition to having a Federal ID number, you will have to have a personal Social Security number. This is used for the purpose of filing individual income tax returns. You will also need to have your own business mailing address that is separate from your home address.

The Importance of Freight Broker Certification:

Certification helps ensure that the public and freight brokers are protected from unlicensed and unqualified individuals who are operating as freight brokers. Certification can help prevent fraud and misrepresentation of freight brokerage services. It also assures that the consumer will receive proper compensation if there are any damages or delays in delivery of their shipment. The certification process also ensures that you are fully knowledgeable about all aspects of freight forwarding, including transportation, customs, documentation, international trade laws, and regulations.

Never Misrepresent Yourself:

Freight brokers cannot misrepresent themselves to obtain business. Freight brokers must also never use the carrier's or freight forwarder's name in order to obtain business. Freight forwarders or air lines will not allow you to use their name in order to gain clients. You are allowed to share your qualifications and experience with others, but you may not represent yourself as being affiliated with that company.

For example, if one of your clients does not know how to properly fill out the air waybill, you may provide assistance with this task. However, you will not be able to change this information. You will also be required to explain all the details surrounding the shipment and make sure that your client has a complete understanding of what is required of them before accepting a shipment.

Another thing that you must always do is make sure that any special requests are clearly explained by the client. If you are making these special requests for a customer, then a copy of the request should be included in the documentation. Special requests would include anything from an oversize load to hazardous materials which require special handling and packaging.

Never Accept Responsibility for Another Company's Policy:

Freight brokers will not accept responsibility for another company's policy or actions. You are always responsible for your own actions and will never hold anyone else accountable. For example, if there are any transportation damages or delays, you will be responsible for making sure that all claims are processed properly. You will also be responsible for filing a complaint with the Transportation Department if any of your clients have a complaint.

You cannot allow your employees to misrepresent themselves or you will be held accountable. Freight brokers may not hold themselves out to be in any way affiliated with the carrier or freight forwarder. You cannot assume responsibility for another company's services, but you may refer clients to them and provide contact information.

Never Make False Claims or Representations:

Freight brokers may not make any false claims regarding their services or their ability to handle a shipment. This would include claiming that they have special access to the freight carriers or that they are affiliated with a particular carrier when they are not. You must never represent yourself as being an agent of the carrier, even if you are a registered agent.

You also cannot accept a shipment if you do not have the capacity to handle it. If you have a full load, you must decline the shipment and refer your client to another freight broker. You should be able to handle the freight forwarder's load within 24 hours or less if possible.

Never Accept or Charge for Services Not Performed:

Freight brokers may not accept payment for services that were never rendered. They will not allow their employees to collect payment for any services that were not provided as well. If a client does not pay for services that were rendered, then it is up to them to collect any unpaid fees. This should be done in accordance with any state laws and regulations regarding collection agencies and debt collection procedures. Freight brokers may charge their clients for fees such as filing charges or late fees, but this must be outlined in writing beforehand in your contract with them.

These are just a few of the freight broker regulations. If you are planning on becoming a freight broker, it is important to understand all the rules and regulations that come with this business. You may also want to consider joining an international association such as the National Transportation Brokers Association (NTBA). This organization will provide you with a code of ethics, definitions, and standards for their members. They will also offer educational programs, conferences, and seminars that can help you learn more about the industry.

You should always remember that you should never misrepresent yourself or your company in any way. It is up to you to protect your clients and yourself from any misrepresentation or false claims by other companies. The industry has set up certification programs in order to help prevent this from happening. If you are interested in becoming a freight broker, it is highly recommended that you pursue certification through one of these programs first. This will ensure that your clients are protected and you have a good reputation within the industry as well as among other freight brokers.

Conclusion

A freight broker business is not difficult to establish. You can make it a full-time income or a part-time venture. The freight broker business is very lucrative as there are many international and domestic freight companies who want to solve their problem of freight carriage.

You will have to invest some money to start this business. The money you spend on the training program and the seminar will be repaid many times in the future. You can decide to run this business on your own or by joining a freight brokerage association or a broker network.

This book has taught you everything about this business. You have learned the preparation and planning of this business, how to find freight carriers, how to contact them, how to build your own shipping network, and how to negotiate prices with these carriers.

Setting up a freight broker business is not difficult at all as we have shown here that anyone can set up a successful freight broker business. However, do not try to take a short cut by not completing the training program and do not try to gain business by making false claims.

It's important that you know what you are getting into. A freight broker business is a good business and you can make a lot of money, but you have to follow the rules and regulations.

Remember that safety is the top priority in this business. You need to maintain safe practices even if it means losing some business. Remember that your reputation will always be on your mind and if your name gets tarnished, it will be difficult for you to get any freight carrier or even a customer.

With these tips, you will be able to establish a successful freight broker business. Good luck and let us know how your business goes.

Made in the USA
Columbia, SC
21 December 2022